ELOQUENT CONCRETE

HOW RUDOLF STEINER EMPLOYED REINFORCED CONCRETE

REX RAAB
ARNE KLINGBORG
ÅKE FANT

RUDOLF STEINER PRESS
LONDON

Cover:
The Goetheanum, West front; detail
viewed from the north-west.
Photograph Hans Gross, Riehen

Illustration on page 1:
The Goetheanum, Eastern stage block:
corner pilaster and roof cornice

Photographs:
Douglas Cole, London:
Illustrations 71, 88.
E. Gmelin, Dornach:
Illustrations 6, 7, 9–12, 19–22, 63, 64,
81, 89, 91, 96, 97, 100, 101, 103,
106, 108, 111, 116, 118.
Hans Gross, Riehen:
Illustrations 18, 23–25, 29, 70, 72–75,
82, 83, 94, 95, 115, 126.
W. Grunder, Basel:
Illustrations 1, 3, 4, 59, 90, 107, 110,
117, 124.
I. Pfabel-Roeder, Dornach:
Illustrations 8, 85, 86, 98, 127, 129.
O. Rietmann, St. Gallen:
Illustrations 2, 14–17, 26, 27, 51–58,
60–62, 93, 99, 102, 112, 114, 119, 122.
W. Roggenkamp, Süderfahrenstedt:
Illustrations 69, 123, 125.
J. Wilkes, Forest Row:
Illustrations 5, 28, 65–68, 76–80, 92,
120, 121.

Layout:
Arne Klingborg, Järna/Sweden

Copyright (illustrations)
Philosophisch-Anthroposophischer
Verlag, Dornach/Switzerland, 1972

Copyright (text)
Rudolf Steiner Press, London 1979

Rudolf Steiner's models and sketches:
All rights with the Rudolf Steiner Nachlassverwaltung,
Dornach/Switzerland
ISBN 0 85440 354 X

Set by Camelot Press, Southampton
Made and printed in Great Britain
by W & J Mackay Limited, Chatham

CONTENTS

THE GOETHEANUM, SCHOOL OF SPIRITUAL SCIENCE, DORNACH, SWITZERLAND
Fine Arts Section

INTRODUCTION

"That building forms might give voice, and that this aim might be fulfilled with concrete as an appropriate building material. Without man's gift for creating forms, without his technical ability, concrete remains formless. Through the exercise of these capacities it might speak an eloquent language unencumbered by words."

For a number of years there has been a growing interest in the architectural work of Rudolf Steiner, the Austrian philosopher, whose buildings at Dornach near Basel in Switzerland have inspired many questions in the minds of practising architects and students throughout the world. Some years ago we took up a number of these questions in our practical work and found that numerous people were interested, from both a practical and an educational viewpoint. As the study sessions and conferences held in England with the help of friends and colleagues from Europe became more frequent, the lack of material in English for those wishing to build up a more personal basis for their study became apparent. It is hoped that the publication of *Eloquent Concrete* will make Rudolf Steiner's work in architecture more accessible to a wider circle in the English-speaking world.

It is difficult to describe a mystery, a chink in a curtain through which something extraordinary is visible, a warmth that is felt when gifted human beings renew their artistic work and transform formless matter into architecture, as in the building of the second Goetheanum. To classify this architecturally is meaningless, to describe it in abstract physical language does not even start to delve into the true nature of the building or bring any clarity to the intense feeling that here is a building that has relevance to present-day social and architectural problems. To study its forms and gestures, to walk around and absorb it from all angles, to learn about the people who built it, and why, are strivings to enter into a dialogue

with the building to which the senses can relate, and recall some of the enthusiasm of its creation.

Today most buildings can be explained away in cold economic and technical language; there is little or no space for the imponderable to enter in, nothing to engage with which asks for a human response, nothing artistic to awaken battered senses. The thousands of people who visit the Goetheanum each year are confronted not with a comfortable recollection of the past in the form of an unusual monument but with a working physical expression of a home for the School of Spiritual Science for which the Goetheanum was built.

Eloquent Concrete is not a book which sets out to form judgements, but sensitively and professionally describes the course of human actions, inspired by Rudolf Steiner, through which the building came into being. The people involved with the building are portrayed with lively clarity and are all named at the end of the text. In a book concerned with architecture this is unusual but here vital in that through working together in free co-operation these individuals, from many different countries and backgrounds, created a social form which demanded an artistic expression in the architecture designed to shelter and support their work and study.

The task of artistically transforming Rudolf Steiner's model into built form presented many structural, technical and procedural problems which, to those involved with building, will have a familiar ring. The interdependence in which individuals sought for solutions which were both innovational and imaginative is truly inspiring and gives rise to the feeling that behind the purely utilitarian act of building there stood an objective to which all could relate with enthusiasm and energy.

It is not as a historical phenomenon that the Goetheanum demands our attention but as a potentially provocative experience leading to the question: What are my talents and capacities and how can I develop them further to reach beyond what I experience now? In this task Rudolf Steiner stands out as an artist of this century who is totally conscious of what he is working with, bringing objectivity and the discipline of spiritual science into the heart of the artistic sphere.

The revealing of the object does not explain the mystery; it is the intangible that fires the imagination to seek out revelation, and it is in this demanding personal search that this book invites participation.

Forest Row, 1979   *Tony Cooper*
                               Christian Thal-Jantzen

PREFACE TO THE SWISS EDITION 1972

The Goetheanum and its position in recent architectural history have become the subject of increasing discussion. Since the transition to the last third of this century, a widespread search has begun for examples and impulses originating in the first third of the century. In the literature dealing with this epoch, the various phases of its development are, however, commonly supplied with neat labels. This practice has tended to obscure the real intentions of the creative pioneers who were then at work. And no one has been more subjected to this treatment than Rudolf Steiner, the designer of the Goetheanum and inaugurator of the School of Spiritual Science in Dornach, Switzerland.

It is true that voices have been raised which designate the Goetheanum as "unclassifiable". Others, however, do not scruple to squeeze this building (construction period 1925–8) into the category of "German Expressionism", "idiosyncratic individualism", "fantasy", "the fantastic", "Symbolism", and of "Art Nouveau". It has even been asked to what extent Steiner was "influenced" by Gaudi, or – casting all chronology to the winds – by Le Corbusier. Such convenient and thoughtless habits will have to be overcome if there is to be any fruitful continuance of the dialogue.

The authors of this volume have gained the impression that many of our contemporaries are not at all happy about this trend in public discussion, whereby an artistic achievement escapes true appreciation and can so easily be cast aside. Such independent-minded people rather feel the need first of all to get to know the object of their study more thoroughly, to let it speak to them more perfectly, before they venture an assessment of their own. For there is always the chance that one may learn something new in the process, which could well lead to a change in one's former views, even to a new confidence and conviction in one's own creative design work. Such unprejudiced persons will gladly avoid premature classifications and prefer to raise questions concerning the nature of the task and the qualities of the particular solution.

In word and picture, our present intention is to give, within its due context, a straightforward description of the architecture in reinforced concrete inaugurated by Rudolf Steiner.

The composition of the book can be regarded as a kind of fugue: one theme is developed by the text, the other by the illustrations, which – as far as is possible through the medium of photography – strive to convey something of the correspondence in space between the architectural centre point and the circumference of the Dornach site at various times of the year and in different moods.

Being active in the artistic field ourselves, we have sought to hold back with ready-made judgements. A study of the subject over many years has served to show us that the mere exercise of the critical faculties falls short of the active inner approach needed in practice.

We hope that a publication attempting to hint at experiences rather than produce something definitive will be welcome at the outset of the last quarter of the century and acceptable both to the general public and to the professional world. We are fully aware that a book is no true substitute for the real thing.

Rex Raab
Arne Klingborg
Åke Fant

MODERN ARCHITECTS MAKE A DISCOVERY

The Goetheanum stands on a slope of the Swiss Jura looking out westward into France. It seems appropriate therefore that the process of conscious discovery of this building by the architectural profession, which set in long after it had been erected, should have received an initial stimulus from within Switzerland.

In August 1960, an entire issue of *Werk*, the well-known Zürich monthly, was devoted to *The Synthesis of the Arts*. This was a notable event. Numbered among its contributions were the results of an *Enquiry into the Integration of the Arts*. All of those consulted — practising architects, sculptors and painters — were agreed that such an integration "would require a common feeling for existence, or even a common 'philosophy of life' ('Weltanschauung')" and that these are lacking at the present time. Yet only a few pages further on, an article by Willy Rotzler, who was at that time the Director of the Museum of Modern Art in Zürich, treats of *The Goetheanum in Dornach as an Example of the Integration of the Arts*. He shows that the School of Spiritual Science known as the Goetheanum did in fact spring from a shared conception of life.

"These buildings," he wrote, "show that an approach to the aims of the 'total work of art' is furthered by particular spiritual conditions, a particular view of life, and also by a particular function of the building layout", and further, that "the unity of the edifice, its striking style, only emerges fully when a community of people imbued with a similar feeling for life attend a stage production which, in its whole spirit, its way of moving and speaking, its scenery and costume design is also an expression of the same will to form. It raises the question as to whether an aim of this sort can be realized at all by a single individual at the drawing board, and, conversely, whether a particular spiritual climate and conviction is not a precondition; whether it does not demand the existence of a community, for which a consistent artistic atmosphere at the same time provides a meaningful centre for its ritual." And Rotzler reaches the conclusion that, in Dornach, "the conception of a total work of art has achieved an unusually pure and powerful expression". These buildings "constitute a bridge between the demand at the beginning of the century for a synthesis of the arts and the renewed postulate of an integration of the arts in our own day".

With this statement Rotzler inaugurated the public discussion of Rudolf Steiner's architecture in reinforced concrete. The deep silence that lay between this rousing call from Zürich and the actual construction of the Goetheanum over three decades earlier had at last been broken.

Werk was not a sole comer. Mario Brunato and Sandro Mendini from Rome had just been to Dornach. They described their impressions in a series of four copiously illustrated issues of *L'architettura* that appeared during the summer months of 1960. They did not only confine themselves to the present Goetheanum in concrete; they also dealt with its predecessor, constructed largely of timber, and with the ancillary buildings grouped around the main structure. Steiner is here described as "one of the most significant representatives of Early German Expressionism". "As a great expressionist, Steiner created masterly works," but, in the opinion of these Italians, "he failed to show new paths for modern architecture".

Three years later an echo with different undertones issued from London. In June 1963 an equally well illustrated contribution by Dennis Sharp on "Rudolf Steiner and the Way to a New Style in Architecture" appeared in *The Architectural Association Journal*. It was part of a larger work. In a revised form, this article forms the last chapter but one of *Modern Architecture*

2   *The Goetheanum, viewed from the banks of the river Birs. 16. 4. 1928.*

3 The Goetheanum from the north-west, in the foreground the "Eurythmeum".

and *Expressionism*, published by Longman in the autumn of 1966 and appearing subsequently in the United States. It is a book that has received wide attention.

For Sharp there was no question that Steiner had shown new paths. Long before the book appeared, this chapter had been expressly selected for early publication, in order to satisfy the need of forward-looking architectural students who were no longer satisfied by the gospel of technology. What causes Sharp some embarrassment, however, is the question as to whether the Goetheanum can be said to come under "German Expressionism" at all.

"Viewing this building objectively, it seems strange that modern architects have ignored it for so long, particularly since the revival of interest in the work of Gaudi in the early 1950s produced so much enthusiasm for this kind of plasticity of form and sculptural monolithy. No doubt a reappraisal of Steiner's contribution to the architecture of Expressionism – and it only just bursts the seams of the date limits given to this phase, 1910 to 1923 – in this post-Ronchamp era is valid, even if its connections with that Master from La Chaux-de-Fonds, which is just down the road from Dornach, are continuously denied. The connections are denied in the face of good evidence, for it was Le Corbusier himself who was speechless (according to Ebbell) when he visited the unfinished shell of the vast 'House of Speech', as Steiner liked to call his project, in 1926–7. Ebbell, when recalling the visit, is reported to have added: 'Someone like that doesn't forget an experience of that sort so soon; it sinks in. I am convinced that he carried it around with him for decades and that it emerged in his chapel.'"

Alongside a number of fresh inaccuracies, a similar chronological adjustment was made in the August–September 1964 issue of the New York

Architectural Forum, a double number that was the swan song of this journal under its old regime. Here, under the heading of *Fantasy*, it was pointed out that the Goetheanum "antedates Le Corbusier's plastic *béton brut* by thirty years or more".

Yet the first to dispense with any form of labelling was Ilse Meissner Reese in her article a year later on "Steiner's Goetheanum at Dornach" in the September 1965 issue of *Progressive Architecture*, another New York journal. "Stylistically," she wrote, "the building is unclassifiable." And she reaches similar conclusions to Rotzler with regard to the value of unity between a given design and the designer's view of life, as exemplified in the Dornach buildings. She too sees the need to bridge the gap between the construction period and the present day. "Whether judged in terms of the twenties or the sixties," she continues, "the Goetheanum is without doubt one of the purest examples of expressionist architecture, for seldom has a structure been designed more specifically to express, to interpret, to reflect a way of life, a philosophy." She further points out: "With few exceptions — Wright's Taliesin West, for example — architects rarely have the opportunity to exercise such absolute control over form and function." And she concludes: "To him [Steiner], architectural forms were organic growths undergoing the same metamorphoses as plant and animal life. His goal was 'to imbue forms with life', to establish 'a harmony of supporting and downward-bearing forces' and to achieve a balanced 'counterpoint of concave and convex architectonic forms.' The static, geometric structures of previous generations, he felt, were not adequate to express his new Spiritual Science. Five lectures, given in 1914 and entitled *Ways to a New Style in Architecture*, outlined Steiner's system of structure and ornamentation and found application in the first Goetheanum, begun in 1913. Tragically, this first building — a vast hollow wood sculpture of rare design interest — was destroyed by fire soon after its completion in 1922. Reinforced concrete was therefore the logical choice for the second Goetheanum, not only because of its fire-resistive qualities, but mostly for its plastic possibilities. These Steiner explored to the fullest with the help of a study model of clay (plasticine), which served as the guide for the erection of the wooden forms into which the concrete was poured. 'Let us try to feel how one thing is connected with another,' he said again and again to his followers, and, in demonstrating this thesis in terms of architecture, he revealed a rare intuitive talent that many trained architects would envy."

Ilse Meissner Reese's text was supported by excellent illustrations by the well-known American architectural photographer, Clemens Kalisher, who had himself independently discovered the Goetheanum in the summer of 1964. Their qualified contribution was headed by an eloquent motto summarizing a cardinal aim of the creator of the work in Dornach: "We should feel the walls as the living negative of the words that are spoken, and the deeds that are done in this building."

A meeting with Hans Scharoun belongs to this sequence of events. It was Whitsun 1962. Scharoun's Philharmonic Hall in Berlin was in course of construction. The opening of the New Church in Wilmersdorf, another district of the city, provided an opportunity for the Christian Community as the client to arrange a symposium at which the designers could answer to their Berlin colleagues. Professor Scharoun, who had agreed to attend after a prior visit to the site, at first listened quietly to the discussion. When he finally made a contribution, he referred to the travelling exhibition which had been promoted by the Goetheanum as part of the Rudolf Steiner centenary

4 *The Goetheanum from the north, in the foreground the ''Glashaus''.*

celebrations and shown in November 1961 at the Berlin Congress Hall. He said that the meeting with Steiner's architectural work which this exhibition had made possible was to him a revelation; a real discovery. He considered the second Goetheanum to be "the most significant building of the first half of the century" and announced his intention of making an early visit to Dornach.

Such meetings and discoveries had been confined thus far to the western and central European worlds. Soon they were to be enhanced by the observations of visitors to the Goetheanum from the Far East.

In the same year, 1926, in which Le Corbusier paid his first visit to the unfinished work in Dornach, Kenji Imai, a young professor of architectural design from Waseda University in Tokyo, was travelling Europe for the first time. Imai had a lively sense for architectural progress in all its forms. On his return to Japan he became one of the chief protagonists of the modern movement as exemplified in Germany, France, Holland and Sweden, and he soon demonstrated in practice his particular attachment to the work of Antonio Gaudi. His impressions of Dornach were of a particular order and reached beneath the surface. At the time of his first visit, the original building was a thing of the past. A palisade of scaffolding poles largely concealed the rising walls of its successor. His meeting with the ancillary buildings – and with the spirit of their creator – served to stimulate a lasting interest. Yet the full impact of his impressions only fully made itself felt four decades later, during his second journey to Europe in the summer of 1963. At last he was able to experience the completed Goetheanum. What he saw of other European architecture that had arisen during the intervening period was a disappointment to him. He had expected to find greater signs of progress, he wrote. This time, on his return to Japan, he saw his chief task in making Steiner and his architectural achievements better known.

He pursued this campaign with every means at his disposal. The introductory passage of an illustrated booklet which he brought out in Tokyo in the spring of 1964 witnesses to the honesty of his approach. The young Japanese architect who undertook a translation admitted that he could not do justice to the literary qualities of the Japanese original. Imai wrote: "I feel bound to take up once again the noble ideas which Rudolf Steiner (1861–1925), the unknown artist, the philosopher who embraced psychology and education, has not ceased to offer our contemporary and future world of architecture.

"Yet the School of Spiritual Science, as his chief architectural creation, is a work divided from the immediate present by a considerable period. Moreover, his entire efforts were at that time displaced by the 'Bauhaus' movement of Dessau, which by the end of 1926 had assumed a brilliant dominion over the modern architectural scene. And yet I am deeply persuaded that Rudolf Steiner's idea, which did not capitulate before the functionalist architects of the day and was therefore buried and forgotten in a welter of scornful criticism, is today still powerfully, quietly, vitally and eternally present."[1]

The Japanese architect then proceeds to outline the result of his researches under a series of headings. Following on the first section, *The Unknown Artist*, come: *The Design of the Goetheanum; About Steiner Himself; The Anthroposophical Society; The Interior of the Present Goetheanum; The Architect who creates Soul-Space; The Letters of Instruction* (this is Imai's happy expression for Steiner's five lectures on *Ways to a New Style in Architecture*); *Building as Speech; Colour Composition; Steiner's Striving and Enthusiasm; The Colossal Human Being who strides*

5   *The Goetheanum from the north-east, in the foreground the "Heizhaus".*

the Middle Way; The Goetheanum and the Ronchamp Chapel; The Interior Life; Macroscopic Building Science. Imai's account culminates in an appeal. "I think it is our task," he concludes, "to contemplate afresh the earnest spirit of Rudolf Steiner that indwells the Goetheanum architecture. I cannot help recognizing that his heart-felt desire to bring love and harmony to humanity, whereby the Goetheanum was to be a sun of peace, is beginning to shine as a great example to our modern architecture, just as he had hoped. In this connection I must point to a peculiarity in all his work. With it the problem of tradition, which seems to dominate the minds of modern architects, recedes completely into the background. I appeal to architects throughout the world to make this Goetheanum Building by Rudolf Steiner — the great philosopher of spiritual science, the artist with the mystical character, who is at the same time an architect — to make this building their present and future friend and to visit it at least once. My wish is that they may find an opportunity to ponder on the nature and value of this edifice and to recognize a genuine and dynamic architectural achievement for what it is. In uttering this wish I will conclude my account."

We have here consulted the opinion of a number of representatives of the contemporary professional world. Most of them only became acquainted with the Goetheanum within the last few years; others have only recently taken long-standing knowledge of the subject a step further and decided to publish their findings. This process has been accompanied by a stream of young visitors to Dornach from the schools of architecture and engineering. For each it has been a journey of discovery, often leading to further research and interesting testimonies of study. Closer inspection of these results reveals a number of common factors:

1. The impression arises of having made a discovery of relevance to the immediate present, despite the comparatively distant construction period.

2. Astonishment is expressed that something which can speak such an immediate and impelling language could have existed so long and yet remain largely unnoticed.

3. Whatever their shade of opinion may be, the discoverers are convinced that an injustice would be done if knowledge of their discovery should longer be withheld from their contemporaries.

4. Not only is it recognized that the building speaks an eloquent and untranslatable language of its own — to which reinforced concrete lends itself as a building material — but also that its very existence is intimately bound up with man's relationship to speech. It is speech itself which serves to mediate between the building and life and to weld them both into a single source of energy.

5. The language of this building speaks directly through perception and feeling to the entire human being. It need not first be subjected to a critical assessment. "One experiences something directly from the forms which it is quite impossible to express in any other way. . . . It really does seem as though one's attention is drawn to these buildings and that something then flows between which has nothing to do with thinking or intellectual processes. . . . The reality is in the experience, and it is a marvellous encouragement to have contact with buildings which have been arrived at through and which speak directly to inner feelings" (Lambert Gibbs, R.I.B.A.).

6. A community existing solely by virtue of the efforts of the individuals comprising it is seen to be a prerequisite for the integration of the arts.

A seventh factor is conspicuous by the absence of something. It strikes the student of this situation that these visitors to the Dornach hill are so preoccupied by the plastic qualities of the buildings they find, that, despite their professional interest, questions touching on the actual design task set by a school of spiritual science and the particular solution that was found for it — indeed, any question of function and technique — scarcely seem to occur to them.

This is merely an observation, not a criticism. An explanation could lie in the shortness of time allowed by the visitors for their tour of inspection. In such a case one would be inclined to concentrate on what seemed to be the essentials and to leave more detailed investigation to a subsequent occasion.

Or might the real explanation lie in a prevalent lack of literature on the subject?

True, the authentic message of the building can only be received — as in the case of any partner to a conversation — in its immediate presence. For such a meeting this book can admittedly be no substitute. On the other hand, the public should be given access to all the relevant facts: the basic ideas out of which the work was conceived; the circumstances under which it arose; the task it had and still has to perform; and its subsequent history. The following sections of this book aim at supplying, as far as the authors were able, this very real need.

The possibility that works of art should speak for themselves in a language of their own was an artistic aim which Rudolf Steiner had always keenly felt. And right at the beginning of his architectural activity he stressed that one is "above all responsible to the judgement of posterity".

Now, sixty years later, such judgement is beginning to be voiced.

It reads, therefore, like a first fulfilment of Steiner's artistic goal, if the utterances of such contemporary architects as have been cited here be compared with the following words spoken in an architectural context as early as 1911 by the creator of the Goetheanum:

"The answer to the question as to whether anthroposophy in a wider sense is understood today does not depend on anything we can say in words, or express in thoughts. It all depends on our pressing on to action."[2]

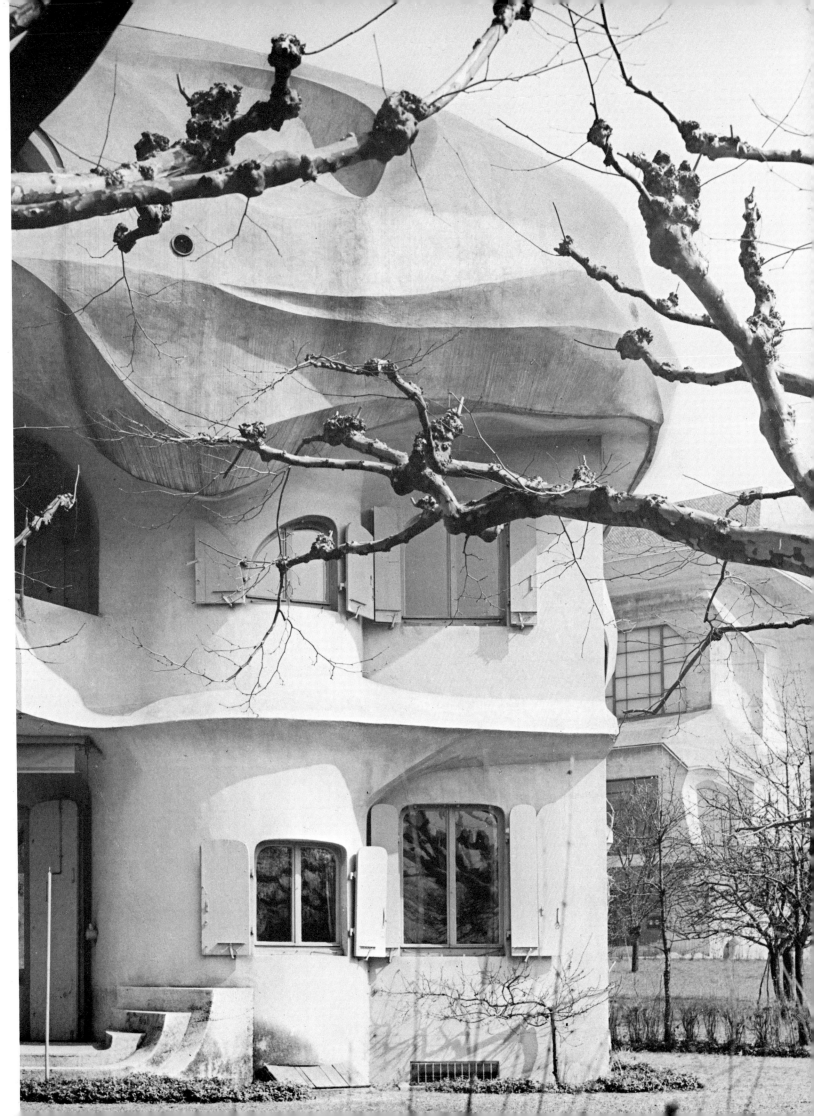

12   The first Goetheanum from the north-east during the construction period. 15. 6. 1914.

13   The plinth, the substructure forming the terrace of the first Goetheanum, after the conflagration (31. 12. 1922). In the rear "Haus de Jaager".

A BUILDING RISES FROM THE ASHES

On the site of the present Goetheanum there once stood another structure — the first to bear this name. Both were designed by Rudolf Steiner. The conception of the first Goetheanum was quite different from that of its successor, which is built entirely in reinforced concrete, as described in detail in the following pages. Viewed from the outside, the original building consisted of two interpenetrating rotundas of unequal diameter constructed in timber. Resting on these cylindrical elements were two corresponding cupolas roofed with slates. At their juncture two wings extended towards the north and south, and a vestibule projected to the west, also built in timber. The entire building rested on a substructure of reinforced concrete. Its construction, begun in 1913, was in all essentials brought to completion by 1922. Its interior and exterior forms could be recognized as variations of a single basic motif.

Its designer described his architectural conception in a public lantern lecture in Berne. "Anthroposophical spiritual science has found a centre for its activity in Dornach, near Basel. This centre, called the Goetheanum, the School of Spiritual Science, came into being as an expression of the expansion of this anthroposophically oriented spiritual science. After spiritual science had been introduced by myself and others — at first in the form of ideas — by lectures given in many different places and countries over a period of years, the inner necessity arose around the year 1909 or 1910 to present the aims of this spiritual science to the souls of our fellow men through other modes of revelation or communication than are to be found in simple thoughts and words.

"And so a sequence of Mystery Dramas I had written came to be produced on the stage — at first in Munich — with the aim of presenting that which anthroposophical spiritual science must convey out of its inner nature. . .

"Certainly the course of history might further be sketched, outlining the essentials of ancient architecture with its elements of load and support; then moving on to the Gothic, to illustrate how architecture emerged from a merely passive support of the load; how by means of pointed arch and ribbed vaulting architectural striving emancipated itself from a sense of weight; and how a transition was found to a living element.

"In Dornach the attempt has been made to develop this living quality further, until we have in fact translated what in earlier architectural styles was merely static and symmetrical into something organic. I am well aware that a great deal can be written from the standpoint of the architecture of the past against such a transition from rigidly geometrical forms to organic forms, that is, to forms which otherwise occur only in living creatures. In our building, however, there are no organic forms imitated in a naturalistic way; rather has the attempt been made to enter into the organic, creative principle of nature.

"This is what we have aspired to in Dornach. The entire building is conceived out of the whole. Every single part is formed individually according to its own place; and it must of necessity be in just that place. As I have said, and despite all that may be raised in objection, the attempt *has* been made here to bring about a transition from purely geometrical, mechanical construction to building in organic forms. This architectural conception could of course be combined with other conceptions, but very little would be achieved — particularly for a creative person. Something like this must arise out of its rudiments. Therefore, when I am asked *how* the single form emerging from the whole is to be experienced, I can only say this: Consider for example a walnut. The walnut has a shell. The nutshell is formed around the nut, around the kernel, by the same laws as brought the nut itself into being. You could not imagine the nutshell other than it is, once the kernel itself is as it is.

"Now consider spiritual science on these lines. The individual brings forth spiritual science out of its own inner impulse and gives it shape in the form of ideas. He composes it in ideas and lives thus inside the whole being of spiritual science. You will forgive me the trivial comparison, but it does clarify how directly, how naïvely one must proceed in wanting to create something like the building in Dornach. One stands within spiritual science as if in a nut-kernel and carries in oneself the laws according to which the nutshell, the building, has to be designed.

"But precisely because anthroposophical spiritual science creates out of the whole, out of a full humanity, it cannot endure the discrepancy of adopting just any architectural style for its centre, and attempting to speak and communicate within that. It is more than mere theory; it is life. And so spiritual science must furnish not only the kernel but also the shell, carried out to the last detail. It must be created out of the same inner laws that generate the words spoken, the Mystery Drama produced or the art of eurythmy performed here. Everything presented in words, that is performed eurythmically or in the Mystery Plays, or whatever else it may be, must ring through the auditorium or assume visible shape in such a way that the very walls give their assent, the paintings in the dome add their approval, as a matter of course; that the eyes take it in as something in which they directly participate. Every column should speak in the same way that the mouth speaks when it gives voice to anthroposophically oriented spiritual science! And precisely because it is at one and the same time science, art and religion, an anthroposophically oriented spiritual science must develop its own conception of architecture, quite distinct from all other architectural styles."[3]

As the first Goetheanum progressed from the planning stage to its final execution, a large group of artists, architects, engineers and craftsmen assembled and set to work with a will to make this plastically conceived building a reality. In due course the building approached completion and by the autumn of 1920 it could be put to use, although it was still unfinished. Then the entire timber superstructure was destroyed by arson on the last day of 1922. How deeply shattered those people were who had helped to build it is evidenced by many eye-witness reports. Heinz Müller, a former Waldorf school teacher from Hamburg, writes of his experiences during the fire, as follows:

"It burned for a long time before anyone was able to see flames from outside. When at last they worked their way out into the open — the lights were still burning in the auditorium — a few dared to climb the western staircase once more and, shielded by the organ loft, took a last look into this great hall. On the blackboard to the right of the speaker's rostrum stood the two verses that Rudolf Steiner had written. I too copied them down. As I wrote the last word, the lights went out and the first flames ate their way in from above. We were called back, as the danger of collapse grew greater by the minute, and shortly afterwards the sparks leapt to all sides as the two cupolas crashed in. Soon the columns, reacting to the heat, began to bend slowly to both sides. They stood like glowing, radiant lilies in the scorching flames. Above the red glow to the west the entrance vestibule held firm. The entire western section, built of the hardest wood, was still intact, and as I climbed the slope up to the carpenter's shop I saw Rudolf Steiner point towards the west and say to those standing near him, 'Impress this moment on your minds.' As I turned around, I saw how the organ pipes were just beginning to glow, colouring the flames green and blue. The terrible splendour of this colour still rose as if in warning against the midnight sky, as the bells of the New Year sounded in the distance."[4]

Concrete in the First Goetheanum

After the burning of the first Goetheanum only its plinth, the substructure of concrete forming the terrace, was still standing. This made it possible for Rudolf Steiner's work in this material to stand out more saliently for a time, although the interplay of wood and concrete could no longer be experienced. At the time of its construction, concrete was already fashionable as a building material. The possibility of its replacing conventional structural materials had been accepted. What was sought primarily for the first Goetheanum was a material that would adapt itself fully to the artistic aim of the building, its will to form. It was recognized that this claim could be fulfilled by employing concrete, a material that can be poured in a liquid state, but then hardens to a stone-like consistency.

Moreover this building project required an adaptation to the natural surroundings. Both of these factors — material and site — found expression later in the words of the architect:

"And now the building on the Dornach hill is taking shape. Its general contours are the first thing to be experienced on the site. It is for this reason that the plinth is constructed of concrete. I have attempted to coax artistic forms from this intractable material, and many have noticed how these forms are an extension of the rocky subsoil; how nature's shapes pass over effortlessly into the forms of the building."[5]

Rudolf Steiner aimed to create a "House of Speech", where every form would express the same fundamental mood. In building it he relied on his own model, in which the interplay of down-bearing and support found diverse expression in its various constructional elements. This striving was manifested most clearly in the timber superstructure, but it was already indicated in the parts executed in concrete.

At the entrances to the north and south and at the main entrance in the west, the visitor gained a first impression of this basic architectural theme (Ill. 14). The forms surrounding the entrance gave visible expression to the fact that the downward-bearing and upward-striving forces held each other in balance. This theme was repeated in various ways throughout the building — for example in the characteristic tripartite form of the doors and windows — thus effecting points of architectonic concentration. At the entrances at ground level it could clearly be seen how the concrete had been worked over after the removal of the formwork. At that time builders were not as interested in the appearance of the concrete immediately after it was poured as they are today. They did not consider that the final effect could be achieved at once through the mould into which it was poured. It was customary instead to work over the rough form by hand as it emerged, using an embossing hammer and chisel.

In keeping with its architectural conception, an axis of symmetry ran through the building, serving to increase the visitor's experience of a flowing dynamic, especially if he entered the building through the main entrance in the west, following this axis.

First of all he stepped into an entrance vestibule, giving access to a double stairway, and found himself surrounded by columns of grey concrete, each growing distinctly wider towards its base, supporting arches. The rich and varied play of light and shade which arose in the entrance vestibule was enhanced by the lighter

14   The first Goetheanum during its construction period. South entrance.

and darker spaces into which the arches opened. The concrete arches themselves revealed a dynamic movement, as the apex of an arch did not always lie on the central axis of its particular opening, but was often displaced to one or the other side of the arch. Through such relationships a festive feeling, a sense of expectancy was aroused in the onlooker, who experienced the static element in arches which attained their highest point on their axis and the dynamic element in arches that were asymmetrical, gesturing to one or the other side (Ill. 15). Behind such arches to the left and right wound the stairways, curving symmetrically to the wooden structure above. The handrails were hollowed into the parapet, so that the hand of a person climbing or descending the stairs could glide along in a protective groove.

In the sweeping staircases of white-coated concrete it could be observed how the elements of load and support found physical form through sculptural treatment and, moreover, it grew apparent that although the surfaces had been worked over, it was not a matter of surface treatment alone. Rather had the entire building – even its model – been plastically conceived. Such modelling was a part of the technical design as well. In a number of places Rudolf Steiner allowed this strongly plastic element to emerge from a strictly architectural setting with particular emphasis, as for example at the lower end of the parapet flanking the stairs, where it concentrated itself into a sculptural newel post. This newel revealed the movement in all three dimensions – going on within the visitor himself (Ill. 16, 18). In the pairs of symmetrically placed stocky piers which supported the landings halfway up the flights of stairs, the dynamics of load-bearing became

15   The first Goetheanum. Interior view at ground floor level. 9. 4. 1915.

visible. Here building technique and art joined hands in an effort to find an artistic solution to a structural problem (Ills. 16, 17, 19).

The colour of the concrete substructure, for the most part grey, mingled with the whitish tone of the coating of stucco on the concrete of the balustrades. Both materials were flooded with tints of reddish and yellowish light, as the steps led past openings glazed with thick yellow glass and ended at terrace level before a great red engraved glass window in the upper vestibule executed in massive carved red beech.

Climbing these stairs, the visitor could reach the interior of the building proper. If, instead, he proceeded through the entrance vestibule at ground level with its welcoming forms and followed the axis of symmetry, he would pass through arches, and arrive, with his back

to the entrance, in a region hardly penetrated by daylight, where the cloakrooms lay. To the left and right ambulatories or curving foyers gave access to the front seats of the auditorium under the great cupola, and to the entrances at the north and south.

In the outer walls of these foyers were windows, two groups of three to each side of the axis of symmetry. These grouped windows repeated the window and entrance motif of the building as a whole. In the centre an arch formed with its apex lying axially; in both flanking windows the apex inclined strongly towards the central window. The foyers were well lit by these windows, as the middle opening rose almost to the ceiling and those to the sides nearly as high. The radiators below the windows had sculpturally treated screens of an off-white coated concrete, which took up

16   The first Goetheanum. West entrance zone, with staircase on north side.

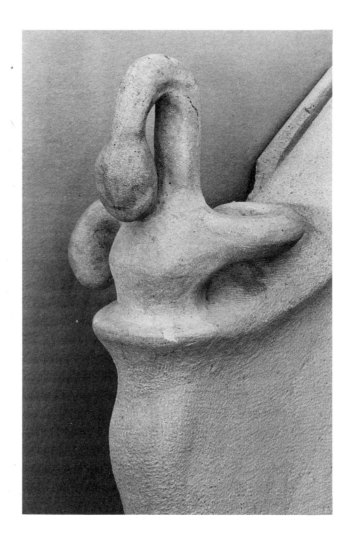

a variation of the theme of the building – the supporting and supported element – here executed with a rich play of tensions, as the modelling assumed a sculptural quality (Ills. 20–25). Despite the unexpected forms of the radiator screens, it could not however be said that they were incompatible with the compositional theme. Their effect was rather that of a cheerful modification of the serious theme of the building.

Heinz Müller, the eye-witness already quoted, recalled a meeting with Rudolf Steiner when the conversation turned to the planning of the lower storey:

"You were present yesterday on the conducted tour of the Goetheanum and heard an architect, a stranger to us, wondering why we had built the entrance and cloakroom in such a way that those who wanted to put away their wraps had to meet those who had just hung up theirs! It is customary to avoid such cross-circulation.

"You see, among anthroposophists this has to be different. They must be given the opportunity to meet as often as possible and gladly greet each other. This is our reason for so disposing the staircases that those arriving at the top approach each other from two sides. One group goes more quickly, another is slower, and it is always possible to meet and greet other people."[4]

In building the first Goetheanum, Rudolf Steiner had already wrestled with sculptural problems and discovered the polarities in sculptural work: on the one hand in stone or stone-like material, on the other hand in wood. He found that in art, forms in wood arise more from a concave hollowing out treatment; whereas in stone the convex element has to be considered, so that

17 *The first Goetheanum. West entrance zone, with staircase on north side. View from below.*

18 *The first Goetheanum. West entrance. Balustrade with newel showing "Motif of Equilibrium".*

the dense rounded mass of the stone itself determines the contour. If any thought is given to these problems, it may be perceived that the various materials do indeed imply such qualities. And a study of the first Goetheanum reveals that its execution was in accordance with this principle. In the concrete substructure two processes can be distinguished, the forms developing as much out of the pouring process as from the subsequent sculpting with hammer and chisel. It will be seen that Rudolf Steiner had progressed to new thoughts about working in concrete, which would find expression in the second Goetheanum and in the architecture of the surrounding buildings.

From the main entrance a short walk in a westerly direction takes the visitor to a circular space at the end of the western approach avenue where five benches of concrete were placed in a semi-circle. They are still to be found there (Ill. 23).

The path is flanked by heel or marking stones of the same period, also of plastically formed concrete, which are inclined towards the building (Ill. 24).

It was from such grappling with the material of the sculptor, accompanied by the architectural impulse, that the first Goetheanum emerged. Its creator believed that the wooden walls, through their treatment in strong relief, and through forms that seemed to expand outwards, not based on anything belonging to the physical world, would take on life and evidence a spiritual dimension. Thus arose "etheric"

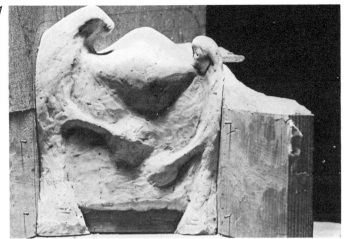

forms, dissolving the sheer physicality of the walls. Here the concern was not merely with gravity, but with the victory over gravity, which was represented by the union of forces in an interplay that assumed plastic form and became the chief motif of the entire building. This only became fully articulate in the wooden part of the building and was varied so consistently that every constructional element, from whatever angle it was viewed, was seen to derive from it. It was not a matter of merely repeating a motif, but, as in a musical composition, of varying the theme again and again, bringing it into new relationships, as was necessary in the manifold subdivisions of the interior. Only in this way was it justified in giving the building the name "Goetheanum". For Steiner had quite consciously linked his work with Goethe's, who, in his studies of metamorphosis, had discovered such transformation and conformity in the organic world.

The concrete part of the building that remained after the conflagration represented but a fraction of the whole composition.

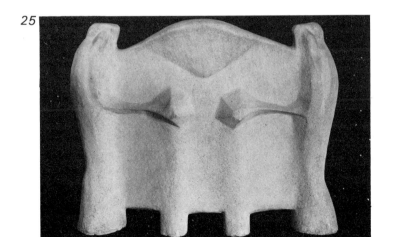

19   The first Goetheanum. Rudolf Steiner's model for the western staircase with landing support. Wax 1913/14.

20, 21, 22   The first Goetheanum. Wax models for radiator screens.

23   Outdoor bench in concrete.

24   Heel or marking stone flanking western approach.

25   The first Goetheanum. Radiator screen executed in concrete, undamaged by the fire.

1. Jan. 1924. Vorm.

The Impulse to Rebuild

Without the least delay Rudolf Steiner took initial steps in making the reconstruction of the Goetheanum possible. As might be expected, much conferring preceded his first written or spoken references to the building to be erected. In March 1923, in the *Goetheanum* weekly, he wrote of the new requirements which this building would have to fulfil as opposed to those of its predecessor. It was evident that another storey would have to be added to provide room for artistic and scientific activities, as well as for the internal needs of the anthroposophical movement. Three months after the fire it was already clear that the new building plan would have to encompass many claims, although the question still remained open as to its actual extent.

In an address to the Goetheanum Association on 17 June of the same year, Rudolf Steiner pointed unequivocally to the attitude that would be essential if such a new building were to arise. With regard to the actual reconstruction, he expressed the view that it would be quite impossible to restore the old building in the same form. This he grounded not merely on aesthetic or historical considerations, which any artist would feel in the face of a work that had been destroyed, but on reasons implicit in anthroposophical morality.

A tremendous capacity for sacrifice had characterized the building of the first Goetheanum, and precisely because of this readiness for sacrifice, because of the enthusiasm behind it, was it able to assume the form it had received. Rudolf Steiner then took up the question of financing, in connection with the insurance on the old building. The moral basis was totally changed by the money paid out of insurance. Alien money predominated over personal offerings, and thus a different attitude would have to be adopted in the restoration, an attitude which he described as tragic. In view of the situation at that time, he pointed out, it was unfortunately impossible to take the radical step of donating the money to some worthy cause or the like, in order to be able to rebuild the Goetheanum solely from the gifts of its friends.

In the following month, the delegates of the Anthroposophical Society gathered in Dornach expressed the hope that Rudolf Steiner would be prepared to take over the reconstruction himself. In addition, they extended him their deepest confidence. Again he spoke of the economics of the matter but also highlighted other aspects in the background: "The building of the Goetheanum cannot be realized with money alone. On the contrary, it must be accomplished with the support of the 'moral funds' of the

Anthroposophical Society. This is the only way. These moral funds must exist."[6]

On 31 December 1923, a year to the day after the loss of the first Goetheanum, Rudolf Steiner presented the *Future Building Plans for Dornach*. On this day he restricted himself largely to the interior design, whilst on the following day he expanded on the exterior. Again he broached the pertinent financial questions, suggesting that a sum of 3 to $3\frac{1}{2}$ million Swiss francs be considered for the reconstruction. He then went into the building conception and repeated what he had written in March of the preceding year concerning space requirements. In particular he brought up the ground plan and questions concerning building materials: "The future Goetheanum should be less a circular building than was its predecessor. You might well say, my dear friends, why don't I place the model before your eyes? True, but you must not forget that this new Goetheanum has to be built in a relatively new material, in concrete. It is extremely difficult to give a concrete structure a suitable and genuinely artistic character and the solution to this problem is very demanding.

"You know that I have already attempted to build a house in a style suited to concrete, the one Dr. Grosheintz put up close by. Now, even though I still can't help believing today that this design is at least to a certain degree – but only to a certain degree – satisfactory for a private house, a second house could not be built to the same plan. In any case, it does not meet the requirements of a Goetheanum, built in the same material. With the new Goetheanum, it will be a case of departing from an essentially circular building and of arriving at something more rectangular, not rounded – an angular building.

"Let us consider the architectural conception of the modest building further down the slope, put up as an eurythmy practice hall, to be on the right lines [see *The Dornach Hill*, p. 109]. Of course, it is executed in another material, but you can see that an angular building has considerable possibilities.

"Naturally, since it is a question of providing stages for eurythmy and the Mystery Dramas, the angular building will have to be combined with the circular. Moreover, the new Goetheanum must have space for its various activities. We shall need studios and lecture rooms as well, for the single small white hall, in which the fire first broke out a year ago, proved to be a space totally inadequate for our purposes. Hence the second Goetheanum will have to be built with a lower level, a ground floor, and an upper level as well. The upper storey will essentially comprise the large auditorium to accommodate audiences during eurythmy, Mystery Drama and other performances. On the ground floor (at terrace level), beneath this auditorium, will be a number of smaller rooms, separated from each other by walls, which will furnish space for artistic and scientific work.

"I am also considering providing space for the purposes of the administration of the General Anthroposophical Society, so that this work can be conducted directly from the Goetheanum.

"Through this architectural conception I would like to solve a certain problem which seems to me to be resolved practically in this way. The ground plan will be drawn so that we have a stage towards the rear with a rounded form. Essentially this stage will form a semi-circle, and it will be encompassed by storage rooms for scenery. The whole structure will be extended to the fore, above into the auditorium and below into the individual working areas, between which a general passageway will lie, enabling a freer movement in this new Goetheanum than was possible in the old. As soon as a visitor stepped into an entrance vestibule of the first Goetheanum, he was inside the building proper. To allow free movement here we should have a heated circulation area, in which there will be ample opportunity for getting into conversation, and from which there will be access to the various rooms at ground (terrace) level.

"A staircase will lead upwards to the main auditorium, giving on to the stage, or, as the case may be, on to the space where a lecture or whatever it may be is being held.

"The practical problem to which I just referred is this: in the old Goetheanum we suffered particularly from the fact that eurythmy rehearsals had to take place directly on stage. Outside visitors were always coming to see what was going on (and we hope they will continue to come in the future), but we required the auditorium for the work itself. Thus it was never possible to make a proper schedule, such as is necessary for rehearsing and for the preparations needed for performances.

"I would like to solve this problem by having at ground level, that is on the lower storey, a stage of precisely the same size as on the upper level. On the upper floor, with identical measurements, it will serve for performances; on the lower floor for rehearsals only. There will thus be a lower practice room for all rehearsals up to the dress-rehearsal, leaving the upper room free at all times. The lower stage will have an ante-room for those rehearsing, where they may sit or wait, whereas the upper stage will open directly into the auditorium and take up the same space as the ground plan of the rectangular part of the building.

"We shall thus gain the possibility of working in these rooms in a really practical way. It will not be necessary to increase the height of the new Goetheanum appreciably as opposed to the old building, as I do not propose to provide it with a cupola again,

but would rather make the attempt of closing it off with a roof composed of a series of planes, which in their spatial interplay will not, I think, be any less attractive aesthetically than a building with cupolas."[6]

Side access was also envisaged, which would develop into wings, whose upper extremity would permit the introduction of skylights.

In the description of the building given here, it is conspicuous that the storey at terrace level is termed the lower or ground floor, whilst the auditorium and stage level is referred to as the first or upper floor. The reader will be reminded here of a touch of Viennese local colour. In Vienna the storey at street level is by no means considered to be the ground floor. There one must climb through many a mezzanine, many a half or in-between storey above street level, before arriving at the "ground floor"! The terrace-structure or base level of the Goetheanum is a kind of parterre or lower storey and not yet the actual ground level. A connoisseur of the building expressed it in this happy way: "The terrace represents a new earth, on which the building rests!"

As in other spheres of life, so in his presentation of this new building plan, Rudolf Steiner proved himself to be a person always prepared to revise his thinking, in order to strike out in a new direction. He said of the old building, that it already belonged to history, and added that by this he meant the hearts of those to whom he was speaking. In 1924 it was no longer possible to build as in 1913, since so much had happened historically in the interim. In putting up the new structure, account had to be taken of the significant development in the art of eurythmy since 1913, which had evolved as an important element of the stagework. In the first Goetheanum the Mystery Plays, concerning themselves with the transformations and inner dramas of the human soul, and the lectures, had provided the basis for stage design. Its successor must make allowance for this third factor.

In his planning, Rudolf Steiner entered boldly into the contrast between concrete and timber construction. "Concrete forms must be quite different. On the one hand, much will have to be done to master this intractable material, so that the eye of the human soul can follow its forms artistically. On the other hand, it will be necessary to create much that will appear to be decorative but in reality arises from the substance of concrete itself, in order to reveal just this material in an artistic light, through painting or sculpture. I would ask you to consider this germinal thought as the reality from which the Goetheanum should grow. I have urged that, as far as the artistic planning of the Goetheanum is concerned, I be allowed to work independently. It will not be possible to take much account of suggestions or advice drawn from other sources, such as have already been offered — naturally with the best of intentions. It will be of no help to say to me, here or there buildings have been put up in concrete, here or there a factory functions rationally, etc. If the Goetheanum is to be realized as a concrete structure, it must have an original conception, and everything achieved up to now in concrete construction offers in reality no basis for what should arise here."[7]

On the following day, 1 January 1924, the exterior design was discussed. Rudolf Steiner explained that the external forms must emerge from the interior in a design compatible with concrete. He then turned his attention to the design of door and window openings in particular, and voiced the opinion that the shaping forces inherent in the forms of the earlier building could come to expression in concrete as well, but in a manner adapted to the material. The "roof planes" would also contribute to these forms by their "pressure" from above, so that weighing and bearing, thrusting and soaring might unite in an artistic form-synthesis of angular shapes. This theme in its angular version would reveal at its centre a part of a pentagon, that is, something trapezium-shaped. Everywhere the intimation of a pentagon, *but nowhere the pentagon itself* (III. 26). He proceeded to speak of further design principles to be realized in the building. For instance, the pilasters incorporated into walls and other supports representing the bearing principle should be developed in this organically conceived building so that they might have the effect of "roots translated into the architectonic", integrating themselves with the lower storeys.

The forms of the building should in principle be simple, mere intimations. If the readiness for sacrifice were still active, so he concluded his presentation, the building would "in a relatively short time be able to rise as a new Goetheanum on the site of the old, even if in a far more primitive, a far simpler form".[7] The term "primitive" might be misunderstood if one did not recall that he had described the first building itself as being a primitive beginning as well.

The Original Model

It was not quite three months later, towards the end of March 1924, that Rudolf Steiner's model for the building was ready to be carried from his studio to the architects' office in the so-called "Glashaus".

A base had been prepared for the model, consisting of a polygonal block of wood 60 mm thick, representing approximately the substructure. (The height of the ground or terrace storey of the original double-domed building had been 5.5 m, not counting the parapet). Glued on to this block was a plywood sheet cut to the shape of the base-line of the superstructure to a scale of 1:100. The material used for the model was a reddish plastic mass from England called Harbutt's Plasticine. Out of this substance the maquette was built up over a hollow form.

The novel appearance of the model showed a decided development when compared with the description given during the reconstitution of the General Anthroposophical Society in 1923. Of initial importance is the fact that the insurance company considered the old substructure to have been unaffected by the fire and assumed therefore that the terrace could be used for a new building. Rudolf Steiner at first acceded to this view, because he did not wish to overtax the resources of the Society and wanted to make rapid progress with the planning. Thus the model grew up from the ground plan of the old superstructure, although in a completely new form.

The contours of the model made obvious the new form given to the auditorium and stage areas. The great hall had now taken on the form of a trapezoid, whilst the stage area had become rectilinear. (For a comparison with the old building, see p. 60.) Three months before, the idea was to make the hall rectilinear and the stage semi-circular. The new step signified a

more interesting development for the auditorium, which adapts itself much better through the trapezoidal form to its function as a spectator area, whilst the stage, through its rectangular form, lent itself to an up-to-date installation. As far as the authors are aware, it was a pioneering deed at that time to make such a large hall trapezium-shaped. Not only do the side walls open out towards the stage opening, but also, as is apparent from the sketches that went with the design, the floor of the hall rises evenly from row to row, starting from the apron stage, and the lofty vaulted ceiling shows the same tendency to expand towards the stage. There arises a trapezoidal space for the audience with a unified character. The later introduction of an orchestra balcony at the rear of the hall rather enhances than disturbs this effect.

One peculiarity of the experience of space in this trapezoidal hall is a foreshortening of depth for the spectator. Not only are the conditions for visibility favourable in a purely optical sense, but each person experiences an increased sense of being a part of what is happening on the stage. To be sure, because of what height and volume, this spatial form presents certain acoustical problems at the outset, and, due to various circumstances, they have not been fully mastered.

The motif that was to have come to expression on the exterior above doors and windows seems at first glance to have completely disappeared in the model, until one comes to realize with amazement that this motif has been translated into the building as a whole.[8]

How did this new conception come about? Did it develop along with the shaping of the model, starting as this did from the contour of the original building? Or did the picture that was clearly present before Steiner's inner eye at Christmas time gradually develop further? Both explanations would seem plausible, for as early as two-and-a-half months before the model appeared,

27 Rudolf Steiner's model for the second Goetheanum, 1:100 scale. Material: Harbutt's Plasticine, reddish brown.

Mid March 1924. The substructure (ground floor with terrace) was not designed until the autumn of 1924.

that is, at New Year's Eve 1924, he gave expression to ideas which have obviously taken form in the model.

"What I would like to achieve is the following. In a similar way to that by which concrete will make its own demands on us, we have here a space roofed over by a series of descending planes, and these are experienced by the eye as exerting a definite pressure. I would like to have this pressure as far as the eye is concerned taken up by the portal and the window surrounds. At the same time I would like it to be apparent that inwardly, spiritually, we are dealing with something that receives us into a portal, or takes in the light as a window, in order to usher it into the inner space. By means of such forms, I would, moreover, like it to be clear that the Goetheanum should be a kind of *shelter for those who come here seeking the spiritual.*"[9] Thus, whatever else one may believe, one thing is abundantly clear, that in his sculpting of the model, Rudolf Steiner proceeded from a firm experience of the interior, for it is the inner architecture that finds decisive expression in the outer aspect.

This can be no accident. When we reflect on this inversion of inner to outer, we recognize that the interior forms of the first Goetheanum are revealed in the exterior of the new building. However, in this case the directional tendency taken by the evolving forms is quite different from that of the first building. There the forms unfold in an interior space and metamorphose through a sculptural sequence from west to east. Here in "outer space" a simple theme deriving from the cube is sounded in the east. This becomes articulated through the more varied forms of the wings, and is completely transformed through the two roof-bearing pillars that flank the auditorium. This pair of pillars bears up the roof in the direction of its highest point and mediates too between the block-like stage section and the less severe, richly sculpted western face. This west front, incorporating the sculptural high-points of the entire building in transmuted form, contains also the four wall openings — no others occur in the maquette — which could hardly be conceived other than they are. The significance of the two columns as supports was already anticipated at the turn of the year.

"It will be possible by this means to create a well-proportioned exterior. One will see at a glance how the load pressing down from above is caught up and how the pillars in their upward striving give adequate support to what is in process of unfolding from within.

"In a balanced adjustment between the forces of load and support lies the significance of an angular building. If we are now to translate this into an organic building, then we shall have in addition in every part a revelation of the indwelling character of the whole. This will be manifested in such a way that the pillars, which, in the old Goetheanum, rose from below upward, will be metamorphosed. They will unfold themselves in the lower storey, in the ground floor, so to speak, like roots (but naturally with an architectonic character). Only thus will the actual pillars be able to rise up into the upper level and develop into supports for the whole. They will then bring the forms of the roof to completion from within outward — not as a flat roof but more allied to the vaulted surfaces of the former domes. The pillars and columns will of course transform themselves into supports, but at the same time bring to expression what in the old Goetheanum was indicated through its rounded form."[9] Thus in addition to a reversal of direction in the horizontal comes a second reversal in the vertical.

One should not forget in this connection that the forms were not given a new cast without reason. It is essential to grasp that the new material simply required a different formal expression. "The forms out of which a style can be created are to a large extent dependent on the material. Because of the relative softness of wood, the old building was able to impress its forms into every detail of the space in which it was fashioned, deriving them from the spirit of the anthroposophic approach. Through using concrete, forms had to be sought by which space itself gives rise to a design appropriate to its own nature, but which is then able to embrace the anthroposophic."[10]

Dr. Ita Wegman, who was Secretary of the General Anthroposophical Society and Rudolf Steiner's personal physician during the final months of his life, reported shortly after his death how he had worked at the model. "At the appointed time, the master put on his white smock, called for the prepared clay and began to work at the model of the new Goetheanum. He laboured feverishly, without real pauses for rest. I was privileged to be present and experienced with amazement and profound awe how the model came into being. In three days it was finished and stood there, unique in its austere, powerful, yet so beautiful forms. From this model we were now to erect the new Goetheanum on the Dornach hill, a building for the anthroposophy of the present and future. Anthroposophy with its friends and enemies needed a building that would take both into account; a building in whose inner spaces a man might devote himself to art and hear the word that anthroposophy has to proclaim; a building whose exterior shows by its form and resistant material that it has the will to stand firm and offer protection."[11]

Though the date in question is not expressly stated, it can be determined with a large measure of probability. A number of years later in the weekly *Das Goetheanum* appeared a report by the poet Albert Steffen *From a Book of Recollections* on a youth conference in Dornach on 17 March 1924. "On the same day," he notes, "I had seen the model of the new Goetheanum in Rudolf Steiner's studio. This creation of his in reddish clay, now completed, worked on in me like a chorale."

Within the ten days preceding 17 March, two days stand out – the 10 and 11 March – on which Rudolf Steiner held no lecture. On 12 March in the morning a lecture was held for the workmen, but the following day was again free of all commitments. It is thus not difficult to see in this period[12] an opportunity for working feverishly for three days "without real pauses for rest".

A few days after the visit of Albert Steffen, when the model was carried down to the "Glashaus" (the glass engraving studio) for the purpose of preparing the plans – this is given as 26 March[13] – its creator remarked to his physician, "It has made a sensation!"

On one further occasion Steiner was to put his hand to the model, this time in the "Glashaus" where the architects' drawing office was installed. An architect working there at the time, Felix Durach, was able to report as eye-witness that a correction was undertaken on the flank of the western part of the eaves. Plasticine was added here in order to give emphasis to the forward-thrusting and receiving gestures alike and thus to achieve a more perfect balance.

28 Rudolf Steiner's model for the second Goetheanum, main entrance front. Only the left side of the model was completed.

29   *Rudolf Steiner's model for the second Goetheanum,*
stage block with north wing.

Before we turn to the planning period, we present here in easily surveyable form a comparison between the various stages of development of the design.

Thus we see that the design went through various transformations. Yet such modification, which belongs to the character of everything organic, need not prevent our recognizing the basic tendency. A pervading principle guiding growth is another aspect of living things. Thus in the terminology employed by Louis Sullivan (who died in 1924) we must speak on the one hand of "morphology" or metamorphosis, on the other hand of "function", which he understood as an attribute of the organic.

The distribution of functions in the Goetheanum

First Goetheanum	*Second Goetheanum*
(As erected in Dornach, 1913–22)	(As intended at the time of the Christmas Conference 1923)
Circular building	"Partly circular, partly angular building."
"Really only a single use possible." (Mystery Drama, lecture or eurythmy.) "The small white hall insufficient."	"Spaces for the various activities." "An auditorium for the audience and spectators at eurythmy, Mystery Drama and other performances." "Rooms for artistic and scientific work." "A space for the Administration of the General Anthroposophical Society." Possibilities for conferences of every kind. "To the rear a stage" and storage space. "A freer movement" than in the first building.
A building with domes	"The roof . . . composed of planes . . . no less attractive aesthetically than a domed building."
Essentially a wooden building.	"It will be possible to derive forms from stubborn concrete which offer something new to an artistic eye."
Rich articulation and shaping of detail.	"A much more primitive, much simpler form."

"The conception of the future building in Dornach" Christmas 1923 (cf. blackboard sketches)	Plasticine Model I : 100 scale March 1924
Auditorium block: "more rectilinear; that is, an angular building".	Auditorium block: trapezoidal form.
Stage: "Essentially a semi-circle."	Stage block: a cubic mass with shaved off corners.
A plastic form adapted to concrete "at the side and main entrances, as also at the window-openings".	The motif is transformed on a grand scale into the building itself.
It is assumed by the authorities that the substructure of the old Goetheanum will be used again for the new building.	The contour of the terrace is not indicated.

may be explained by the many kinds of activity that were to be carried on under a single roof. Although such compact planning in a building of over 110,000 cubic metres of useable space no longer astonishes us, given the current attitude to planning, we would normally justify it by the exigencies of servicing, economics or site boundaries. At that period, however, an analysis of such varying functions would have led most architects to group them in more than one building. But it is precisely the concentration of functions that is characteristic and decisive in Rudolf Steiner's approach.

Just as it is the task of a School for Spiritual Science to explore the relation between the various fields of knowledge and show that these can be embraced by a central, all-enlightening "ecological" knowledge of man and universe, so should the chief building serving this goal also be "comprehensive". The individual sections of this school aim to avoid getting lost in specialization or fragmentation, seeking to unfold an organic collaboration "under one roof".

If the incorporation of still other fields of activity should lead in time to the erection of corresponding ancillary buildings, this would not mean a departure from the comprehensive line, for the same form-principle would permeate all the buildings and arrange them in a manner suited to their function. Initially, however, the centre of gravity which would hold everything together had to be re-established in the new Goetheanum in a transformed and heightened form.

The Building Permit

As soon as the model was completed, the architects led by Ernst Aisenpreis set to work measuring it up as a basis for detailed planning. It formed the basis for the preliminary building application at the end of April, which meant a planning period of just five weeks. The fact that Rudolf Steiner had to include the old terrace structure in this request had as a consequence that the eastern part of the building with its blocky character rose up abruptly from ground level. The terrace of the first Goetheanum had not extended around the whole building, but terminated at the wings before reaching the eastern end.

Accompanying a set of preliminary drawings submitted on the 20 May 1924, was the following brief but significant letter, which presented fundamental points of view that would guide the erection of the second Goetheanum.

To the Central Administration
of the Canton Solothurn
in Solothurn

In accordance with a summons from the esteemed President of the Building Department in his letter of 19 February 1923, we herewith present the plans for the new Goetheanum to the Central Administration for due consideration.

On receipt of your approval we intend to begin with the rebuilding without delay and to proceed with it as quickly as possible.

The new building will stand directly on the site of the old. With regard to the construction of the building as a whole, we bring to your attention that it is to be executed as a solid structure and that all constructional parts, all floors and bearing walls, as well as the roof trusses will be carried out in reinforced concrete. We plan to employ a purely steel construction for the support of the floor of the main stage alone. — Timber will be used nowhere as a constructional element in the building, but exclusively for doors, windows, flooring and floor construction over solid slab floors, for rafters and for fixtures and cladding. As roofing material the same Norwegian slate as was used on the old Goetheanum is to be employed.

We shall provide exits as to size and number in accordance with the requirements of the building codes.

We are convinced that the entire building, when completed in this type of construction, will be able to meet all requirements as to fire safety to an unusual degree. We trust therefore that the Central Administrative Council will be in agreement with the execution of the new Goetheanum according to the enclosed plans.

Most respectfully,

Dr. Rudolf Steiner   E. Aisenpreis

Enclosures: 10 Drawings.

The drawings enclosed clearly betray the manner of Hermann Ranzenberger, who had come to Dornach from Swabia as early as July 1914 to work in the architects' office. We note here the devotion in particular to what remained of the old Goetheanum. We can sense the struggle to rhyme the old terrace structure with the new building conception. Nevertheless, we only see confirmed the fact that the old terrace was in every respect unsuited to form a part of the new building. Not only had it suffered irreparable damage from the effects of heat, but it was found that the erection of the new structure made its removal unavoidable on technical and constructional grounds. In any case the design demanded, from the artistic side, a uniform stylistic treatment of all the elements of the building. Perhaps for these reasons we have to consider this preliminary building application to have been at least in part a feeler as to how officials and neighbours would react to the building plans.

In the minutes of the Administrative Council of the Canton Solothurn on 9 September 1924 it is noted:

"The Solothurn Chapter of the Association of Swiss Engineers and Architects, appointed to examine the project and give their expert opinion, expressed themselves as follows with regard to the preservation of the national interest (Heimatschutz):

" 'Concerning the forms used in this building project, it must be established that these cannot in any way be compared to the traditional forms of building used in our country, as the building exterior conforms to no known style. The question then is this: how would the building relate itself to the surrounding villages and to the landscape? To this we remark that as a consequence of its considerable distance from Dornach and Arlesheim, the building, together with the dwellings of the anthroposophists already standing in the vicinity, which have been built in a character similar to that of the projected temple, must be considered as an isolated group of buildings. Numerous stands of trees separate the settlement from Dornach. The details of the building do not come into visibility until one is close at hand, so that the group of buildings will not affect the surrounding localities in the sense of the laws protecting the national character. (Heimatschutz)

" 'Observed from a greater distance, the building will present nothing but a silhouette. Indeed, in our opinion this will be less obtrusive to the view than was the

former domed structure. The building will fit better into the landscape, so long as care is used in providing the right colour treatment for roof surfaces (slate covering) and facades.

" 'To be sure, the building could never be considered typical for this area. Only the future will reveal whether we can come to terms with building forms of this nature.'

"On the other hand, petitions objecting to the exterior architecture of the building have been submitted by the Swiss Association for the Protection of the National Interest (Heimatschutz), the Union of Swiss Architects, the Society of Swiss Painters, Sculptors and Architects, as well as the Swiss Pro Compagna Organization for the Cultivation of the Landscape. The Administrative Council of Canton Baselland has joined in the request that everything

31 From the building application of 20. 5. 1924: ground floor plan with terrace of the first Goetheanum.

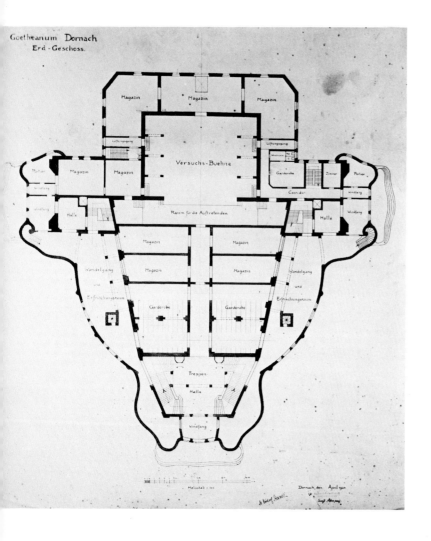

and roof surfaces would receive a tone in keeping with the landscape. The objections to the height of the building would be met, according to assurances given by Dr. Steiner, by an appreciable reduction.

"In view of the fact that the village of Dornach has given its approval for the erection of the building by a large majority, that the safety of the building and the neighbouring village of Arlesheim is assured as far as fire and police regulations are concerned, that a better adaptation to the landscape will come about through reduction of the height and the colour of the façades and roof surfaces, and out of respect for the opinion of the Solothurn Chapter of the Association of Swiss Engineers and Architects, it is not deemed proper, according to paragraph 276 of the preamble to the law, to oppose the erection of the building.

"It is accordingly *resolved*:

The *erection of the new Goetheanum* is approved *under the following conditions*:

1. The proposed plans are to be changed according to the wishes of the village of Dornach and the assurances given. The revised plans are to be submitted to the Building Department for approval.

2. The calculations required for the construction of the building are to be submitted. The Building Department is to have these analysed at the expense of the Society. It can demand suspension of construction, should the necessary safeguards not be included.

3. A fireproof curtain is to be installed between the auditorium and the stage and a ventilation system provided for the stage area. The installation is subject to the approval of the inspector for the fire insurance company. A similar restriction applies to

should be done to prevent the disfiguring of the landscape.

"During an inspection of the building site, the Administrative Council was informed as to the form the structure would take. Assurances were given on this occasion that the rear part of the building would receive greater embellishment, according to the wishes of the Dornach Rural District Council. In addition the façades the approval of fire-extinguishing equipment and the heating system.

4. The colour treatment of the façade and the roof surfaces is to be adapted to the landscape. Before such work is undertaken, proposals in this regard are to be submitted to the Building Department.

The Deputy
for the Secretary of State

(signed) Fr. Kiefer

Building Department (5)
   Inspector for Building Insurance
   Magistrate's Office, Dornach
   Goetheanum Association, Dornach.''

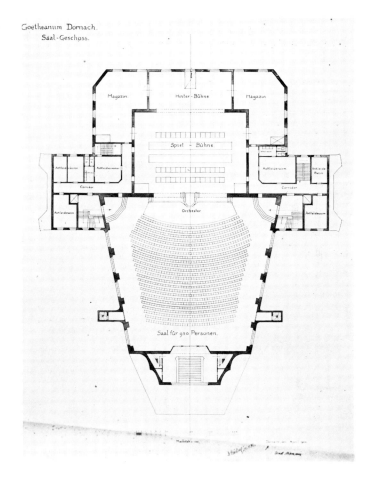

Detailed Planning

Another Swabian architect, Ernst Aisenpreis, who had played a leading part in the Dornach building activity from 1914 onward, had become Rudolf Steiner's valued collaborator and a trusted adviser in building matters. In his capacity as leader of the planning office at the Goetheanum, he had arrived at the following agreement with the engineering firm of Leuprecht and Ebbell in Basel as early as the preceding June.

30 June 1924

Messrs. Leuprecht & Ebbell
Civil Engineers
Basel, Wallstrasse 24

We forward to you herewith a copy of the plans for the reconstruction of the Goetheanum, so that you may inform yourselves in advance. We assume it will be best to start with the foundations for the stage block and the north wing, in particular the latter, since here the foundations will have to be taken to a greater depth owing to the original slope of the ground.

We would ask you to restrict these plans *at first exclusively* to your own personal use, and as far as possible to let no one, particularly persons un-

33   One of two sketches by Rudolf Steiner for the alteration to the stage block.

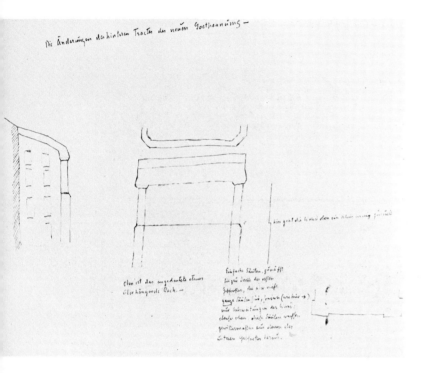

sympathetic to our aims, gain insight into them.

We will contact you in a few days with regard to the test cube.

Finally, with a view to commissioning you with the calculations, kindly send us a contract such as is customarily used in Basel. The details can then be agreed on the basis of such a draft contract.

Most respectfully,
per A.

Enclosed: 10 sheets of drawings.

In accordance with the conditions stated by the Administrative Council, a modification of the plans was

undertaken. The original concept, which called for a new building higher than its predecessor, meant — as can be deduced from the longitudinal section and from the correspondence — that there was altitude to spare. These reserves were shown to be justified, for they permitted the required reduction without the proportions required by the model being significantly affected. This is apparent from the illustrations accompanying this text. Although the finally adopted height of the new terrace compared with the old one showed a reduction of one metre (4·5 m as opposed to 5·5 m), in judging the impression produced by the superstructure and its treatment we can leave this substructure out of consideration. The effective height of the terrace in both structures does not in any case represent a constant, as the ground was not completely levelled. The number of steps at the various entrances is not the same, and differences in the order of 600 mm occur in the terrace height, measured from the ground to the upper edge of the balustrade. Thus one reads off the effective height of both the old and the new Goetheanum from the terrace (or balustrade) level upward and downward (considering these measurements as two separate components). If we now take into consideration the sculptural character of the 1:100 scale model (maximum height without the terrace block 328 mm, minimum height 324 mm or an average of 326 mm) then in the final settling of the height of the superstructure as executed at 32 m above terrace level, it is a matter of a reduction, compared with the model, of 400 mm to a maximum of 800 mm or an average of 600 mm. The height of the terrace above ground level varies between 4·9 and 5·5 or an average of 5·2 m. Accordingly the total average height amounts to $32 + 5·2 = 37·2$ metres (III. 45).

To meet the objections to the eastern end of the building, Rudolf Steiner added pilasters at the corners and a cornice at the roof, whereas the eastern block had previously only been bevelled off. He took the opportunity to introduce a characteristic refinement in the design. This consisted in setting back the whole of the east wall and forming a ledge halfway up the façade, by means of which a threefold division was also indicated at the eastern end between terrace structure, intermediate zone and upper part with its crowning cornice.

A closer inspection of the terrace revealed the extent of the fire damage, and since the new superstructure had turned out to be so fundamentally different in bulk and character, it was not long before a more suitable storey at ground level, enclosing the stage block as well, was designed to replace it.

With these alterations, a revised building application was submitted to the authorities on 11 November 1924. Whereas the effect of the drawings in the preliminary application had been more picturesque, the second application seemed to have become more ordered, serene and defined, this time owing to Hermann Moser's style of presentation and sense of detail. At the same time the first set of calculations by the structural engineers was handed in. The rest followed at regular intervals, so that as early as 1 December the Building Department issued the final permit.

The Terrace

In retrospect it seems hard to believe that the terrace storey was not an integral part of the design from its inception in March 1924. It is a most happy solution. Through it the building received a plinth just right in scale and character and at the same time a convincing transition to the site on which it stands.

34   From the second building application of 11. 11. 1924: south elevation.

35   From the second building application of 11. 11. 1924: perspective sketch of the main entrance front.

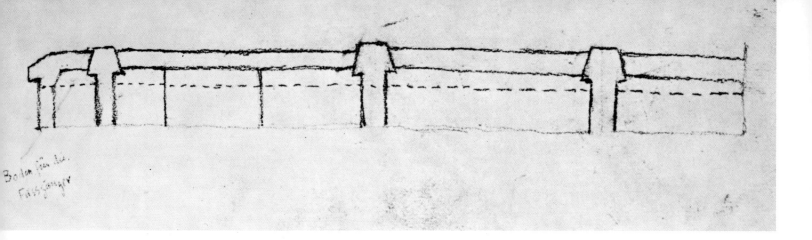

This terrace achieved its ultimate, matured contour in two stages. A sketch by Rudolf Steiner (Ill. 36) conveys in its proportions and details a sufficient idea of the intentions of the design, although it was not drawn precisely to scale. Before one could proceed to the working drawings, the sketch needed elaboration. But this at first admitted of different interpretations.

Illustrations 37, 38 and 39, which shed light on the issue in question, show the outline of terrace and superstructure on plan, the first at the time of the preliminary application on 20 May 1924, the second in the building application of 11 November 1924, and the third as they were actually constructed between 1925 and 1928.

From this emerges an interesting fact as to the shaping of the ground plan. The superstructure and terrace, as built, are happily adjusted to each other. The relationship is established to begin with by concentric circles, whose common centre is the speaker's rostrum in the large auditorium. If the circle circumscribing the superstructure can be said to have its source chiefly in the harmonious proportions of the first Goetheanum, so does the larger circle, which exactly circumscribes the angles of the terrace plan, show itself to be a conscious and necessary correction made in the course of the planning. The ratio of the two radii to one another betrays no obvious law or significance – it lies between 3:4 and 9:13 – and does not encourage the search for mystical meanings or the like. The planning stage we have now described, however, had not yet been arrived at by November 1924, as far as the terrace structure is concerned.

The enclosing walls of the terrace, polygonal on plan, are capped by a plain parapet, interrupted or contained at the entrances to the west, north and south by characteristic squat pylon-like piers. In Rudolf

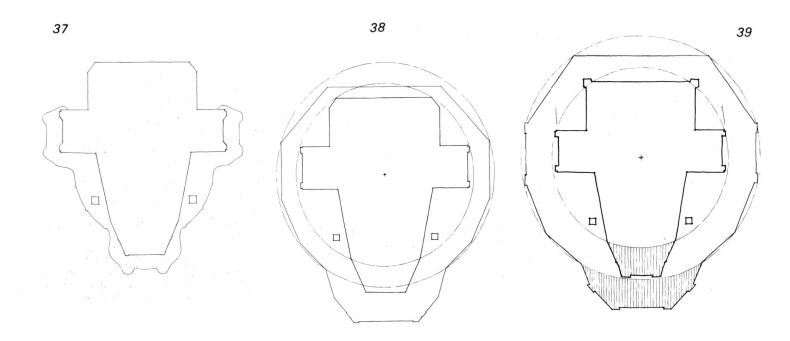

37   38   39

58

Steiner's sketch (Ill. 36) showing the terrace as viewed from the south, a dotted line was marked in, to which the note "floor level for pedestrians" was added. This line is sketched *beneath* the lower edge of the simple parapet moulding capping the terrace.

The sketch, which could hardly have been made before October 1924, allows of two interpretations, since no measurements were given.

a. We could interpret it as a sketch in exact proportion and carry it out literally, i.e. if the terrace together with its parapet is about 6 m high, then the capping would be about 1·5 m.

b. We could attach greater importance to the dotted line introduced by Rudolf Steiner as the "floor level for pedestrians". This would *alter the relation between the parapet and the total height of the terrace structure.* In this way the height of the flat roof of the terrace, where the public is to walk, does indeed come to lie below the bottom edge of the parapet. The moulding or profile of the parapet, however, as viewed from outside, would thus only be about 700 mm high, since the parapet itself, as seen from the terrace, could not well be higher than 1 m.

In the second building application of November 1924, the 1:100 scale drawing showing the south elevation has strangely enough *adopted the second interpretation b* (Ill. 40). As a result the parapet appears far too delicate for the massive superstructure. And, more important still, the well-proportioned piers with their trapezium-shaped tops shown in the original sketch are reduced to a painful, even ludicrous, degree. Hence interpretation *b* was demonstrated to be false. Nevertheless, despite the discrepancies in it, Rudolf Steiner generously signed all the drawings for the building application, since its acceptance was

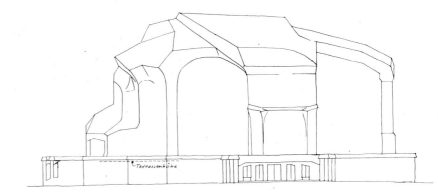

40 From the second building application of 11. 11. 1924: sketch of south elevation.

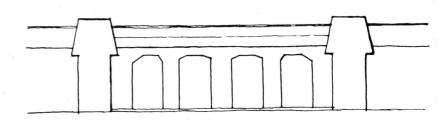

41 Outline sketch of the south entrance as executed.

becoming ever more urgent. Subsequently, however, the terrace with its parapet was worked out in accordance with his original sketch, which was seen to have the right proportions. Reflecting the real size of the parapet moulding, in actual construction the "floor level for pedestrians" was made to lie *above and not lower than* its under edge. In practice this whole problem may appear of mere academic significance. But it was in this way that this masterly terrace came into being, whose proportions convince the eye that such a towering superstructure can well rest upon it.

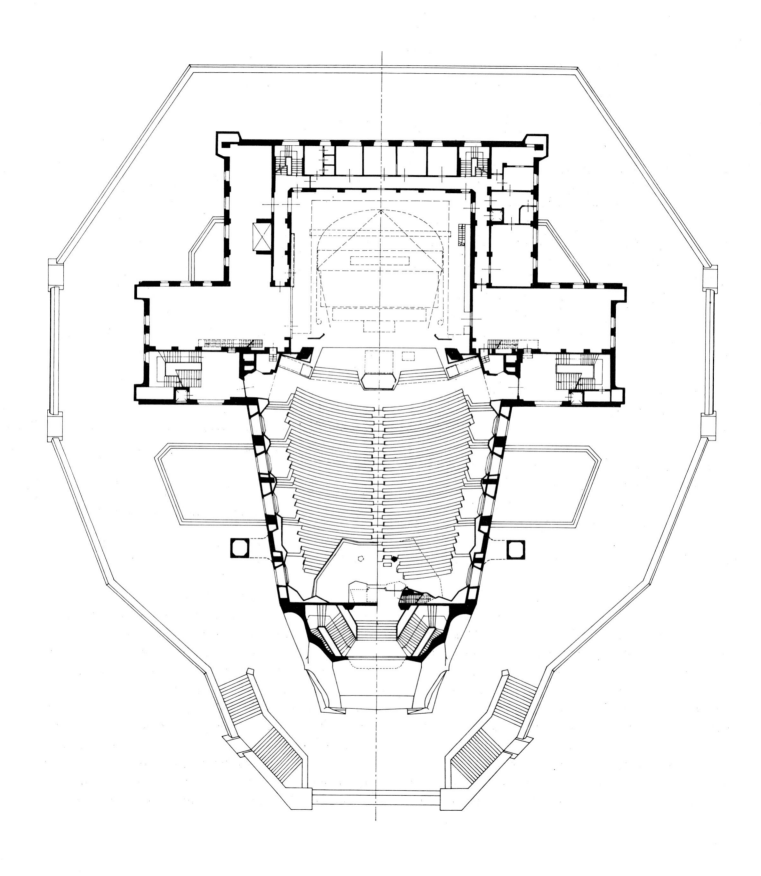

42   The second Goetheanum. Plan at auditorium level.
Seating accommodation for approx. 1100 persons.

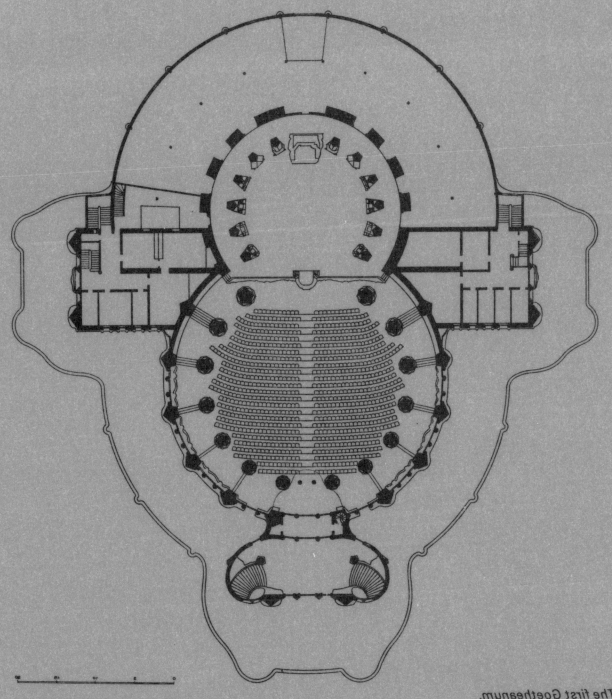

43   The first Goetheanum.
Plan at auditorium level.
Seating accommodation for
approx. 900 persons.

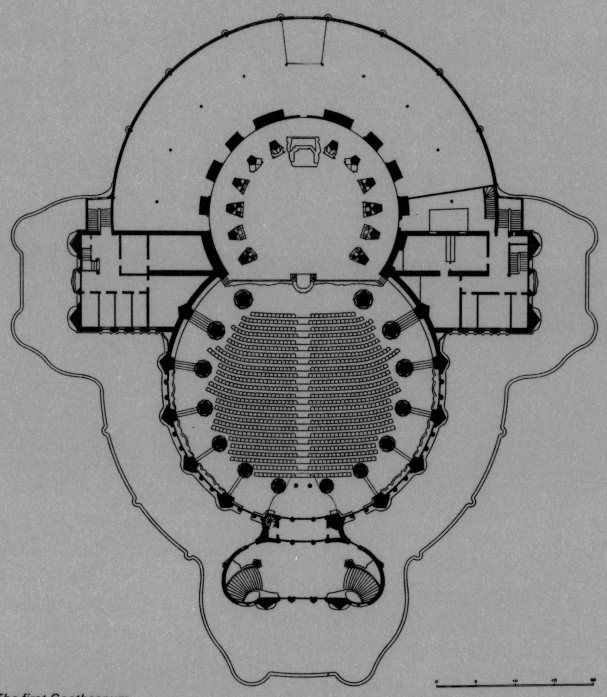

43 The first Goetheanum.
Plan at auditorium level.
Seating accommodation for
approx. 900 persons.

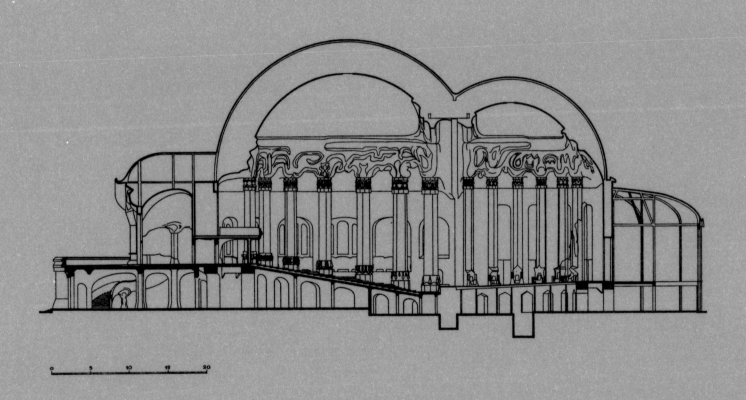

44 The first Goetheanum. Longitudinal section.

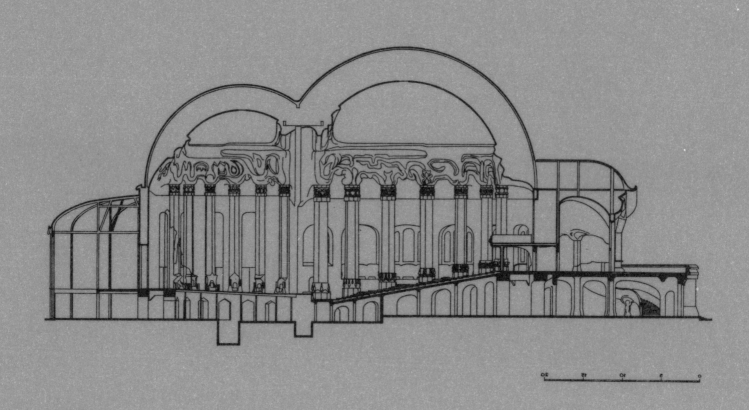

44   The first Goetheanum. Longitudinal section.

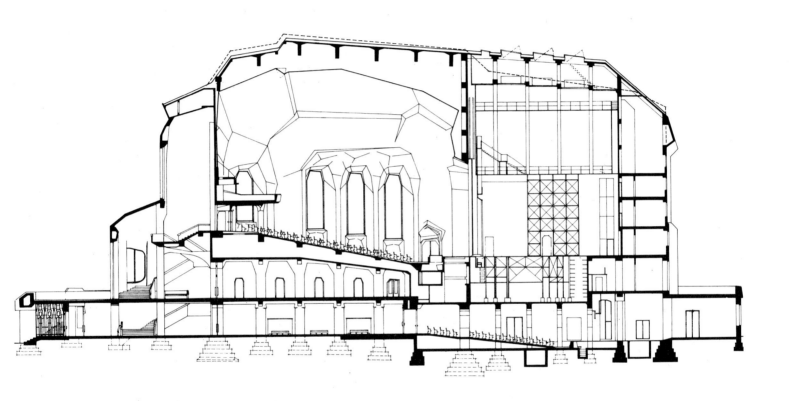

45 *The second Goetheanum. Longitudinal section. The dotted roof line represents the average height of the original model.*

Co-workers – Co-responsibility

The plans made public through the local press during the first half of 1924 were by no means fully matured. This is understandable when dealing with a building that was in so many ways breaking new ground. As far as the critics of the project were concerned, however, this fact represented a weakness. In the case of specialists who were not directly involved in the project, there was no standard by which they might judge with any confidence what there was in it belonging to the future, that must simply be allowed to evolve further, and what required possible revision. The study of the details of the project that ensued, when it did not proceed from mere opposition, led to much well-meaning criticism. It also brought about a number of improvements where obvious but less significant defects were still to be found in the planning, such as in the placement of windows.

Ernst Fiechter, a native Basler who was professor of architecture in Stuttgart, had a number of positive suggestions to make as he struggled to understand the new artistic goals he encountered here. He was in favour of carrying out the project.[14] In judging this whole process, it is necessary to be clear that Rudolf Steiner himself had to be absent much of the time from the scene of action. Only someone who is aware of his other accomplishments in many fields and in many lands at the same time will know how to value the degree of his involvement in the building project. It was clearly in keeping with his wishes that his co-workers were placed largely on their own responsibility and that in the detailing they had to feel their way forward across unfamiliar ground. It illustrates clearly how his way of working, how his relation to the task in hand and to his fellow men, distinguishes itself from that of other outstanding innovators in twentieth-century architecture. Whereas they often treated their co-workers as uncomprehending subordinates, Steiner's attitude always produced encouragement, even a feeling of having a share in his creation. He had faith in a process of ripening. Thus he did not intrude too soon nor unnecessarily into the process, but just at the right moment contributed a new design solution, a new impulse, in order to help things along. One has the impression that this type of collaboration did not cease with his death. In the case we are considering, the change that had taken place between the initial application of May 1924 and the completed project represents a significant stride in the quality of the effort, although from beginning to end it was a matter of faithful execution of an unaltered sketch model.

The working out of the design proceeded slowly at first. A major talent of Aisenpreis as architect in charge showed itself in the skill with which he drew together a team of architects, engineers, sculptors and workmen. With the support of these co-workers, who owed their artistic inspiration and activity to the creator of the Goetheanum, the completion of the building could be carried out in his spirit.

The firm of Siemens had offered their services soon after the catastrophe of the fire and entered actively into the planning on 30 May 1924. They proposed a modern stage with up-to-date technical and electrical equipment, horizontal soffits with a diorama and coloured lighting, and were prepared to send a representative.

As early as the time of the first Goetheanum with its circular stage adapted solely to the Mystery Dramas, Rudolf Steiner had worked with light sources and had insisted on the need for a colour keyboard – such as was developed industrially forty years later – in order to make possible finer and finer transitions in the coloured lighting. He displayed mastery in what amounts to a new art, for instance in handling the effects of coloured light on the colours of costumes.

If we compare the semi-circular or apsidal stage as postulated at Christmas 1923 with the almost square stage of the model, it is apparent that Rudolf Steiner had modified the idea of a "Stage for Mysteries". In its stead a more technically equipped stage was envisioned. This would facilitate scene-changing and the development of coloured lighting. The new stage plan, therefore, anticipated the possibility of realizing what he set forth a few months later concerning the decorative aspects of staging and stylization through colour and light. For it was between 5 and 23 September 1924 that the comprehensive, remarkably vivid and one must say epoch-making lecture cycle on speech-formation and dramatic art was given. It might be added that he found a correspondence to the reality of soul and spirit in a certain confrontation between actor and spectator, which militates against the concept of total theatre, unpopular as this may sound.

The planning of the interior brought new demands, concerning which he was kept informed by Ernst Aisenpreis. These called first for an increase in the wings to north and south – as compared to the model – of up to three metres, to which Steiner gave his approval. The change permitted the inclusion of two side-stage areas in the wings instead of changing rooms for the actors. The well-known stage designer, Professor Hans Wildermann, as well as the architect Hermann Ranzenberger, independently hit on this possibility. In addition it appeared to the technicians from the Maschinenfabrik Wiesbaden, a technical equipment works, who were called in as advisers, that it would be necessary to raise the eastern end together with its roof construction. These negotiations took place at the turn of the year. On 30 January 1925 the step in the roof contour, still evident in the longitudinal section, was finally and totally eliminated. Those acquainted with the qualities of the original design could not help regretting this development. From the later drawings it is clear that some of the architects were still battling for an outer impression more in keeping with the model. In the interests of truth, however, it must be emphasized that the creator and builder of the Goetheanum himself collaborated in this measure from his sickbed. He had the intention of making a further model, not only of the interior of the auditorium, but also of this eastern stage block, in order to clarify his sketches in three-dimensional practice. Posterity may rest assured that the building now to be seen on the Dornach hill is a worthy translation and execution of Rudolf Steiner's intentions. Any alterations which it proved necessary to make are basically of a subordinate nature when measured by the model.

As soon as the model for the building was made available, the possibility had been considered of installing the giant wooden sculpture, which Rudolf Steiner had carved for the first Goetheanum, on the new stage, in accordance with the original intention. Later events showed that this idea was abandoned, however, and by the originator himself. We can point to the fact that he spoke of a room to be specially designed for the sculpture, which, according to a remark made in June 1924, would be the only panelled room in the entire building. From a letter dated 22 April 1925, sent from the planning office to Leuprecht and Ebbell, we can see that shortly after his death plans including a cross section of the "Hall for the Sculptural Group" had been submitted for calculation purposes. To be sure, a final decision as to the place where the sculpture was to be displayed was not made for two further years. For the time being the eastern strip of the stage floor too had been worked out accordingly in reinforced concrete, in order to take this 20 ton, 9 m high object carved in massive laminated wood, even though the problems involved in meeting fire regulations on the stage itself were really beyond solution. Simultaneously, therefore, the planning of a separate room for the sculpture was going on. The fact that this room was actually used to house the "Sculptural Group" underlines more clearly that the second Goetheanum had another task to fulfil than its predecessor. The sacrifice had to be made in full consciousness. What had been conceived as the culmination of the interior of the original building – the form of man – would now seem to stand to one side.

Early in 1925 the building site, quiescent for just over two years, awoke to activity. Building began anew. Admittedly, the first step took the form of demolition. The inadequate and damaged terrace structure and a large part of the old concrete foundations had to be dynamited and cleared away before foundations and a terrace for the new building could take their place. From his rooms in the carpenters' shop, where despite his weakened condition he was tirelessly at work, Rudolf Steiner could hear the blasting and the din of the site work. But it was not granted him to go on supervising his architectural creation. He died on 30 March 1925. His trusted co-workers laboured on, however, with undiminished determination.

From the archives of the Goetheanum for the years 1924–5 it can be seen that a large number of people offered their services to the "New Goetheanum". Letters applying for work on the new site also reached Dornach from abroad. Many of these workers had already been active in Dornach before, and one can detect in the joy they found in their job the inspiring influence of Rudolf Steiner. From the year 1920, at their request, he had held lectures for the workmen, and this had wakened a mood of trust among them.

The working drawings could not be derived directly from the original 1 : 100 scale model in plasticine. To arrive at the necessary degree of engineering precision for calculations and formwork, a model, five times larger, to 1 : 20 scale, was set up in the planning office. The differing sections and elevations taken from this model over a period of time, demonstrate how the architects and sculptors were struggling not only towards the right stylization in concrete for this architectural modelling, but also towards the right proportions within which this modelling would have to unfold. The particularly demanding shapes of the west front, for example, did not reach a stage fit for execution before Carl Kemper had been given permission by the architect-in-charge to go on working at them – a course which had the approval of Albert Steffen, the President of the General Anthroposophical Society. Kemper's accomplishment can only be judged by comparing the treatment of the projecting western staircase as it stands today with the unsatisfactory architects'

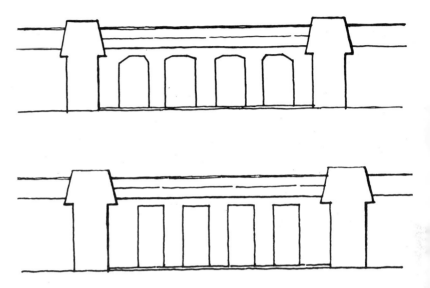

drawings of that earlier period. The 1:20 scale model has been destroyed long since.

In order to *maintain the impression made by* the 1:100 scale design model, after enlargement, Kemper set to work anew on the 1:20 scale working model. He was able to distinguish with sensitivity what there was in the design that had only been intimated and thus needed further working out. His experience over the years had qualified him to take on this responsible task. The window openings to the north and south of the group-of-three at terrace level only reached their present vigorous, yet elegant character through his sculptural rendering. A significant contribution was his broadening of the lintel over the rectangular middle opening, by which a decidedly more balanced proportion was achieved.

He also made corrections in the great western red glazed window opening at auditorium level in the spirit of the design. The relation between the roof section and the total height was skilfully modified over against the model without sacrificing their proportions. In this regard we must recall that the total width of the wings had been increased.

Not only were the ultimate forms for the west front, then, determined by this architectural sculptor, and brought to their artistic culmination, but he also produced a small model revising former suggestions for the flights of steps in the western staircase, and this was finally adopted.

In designing the south staircase, Kemper sought to do justice to the spirit of Rudolf Steiner's intentions. The sculptural quality of the exterior was captured in miniature on the solid balustrades, in part by means of stucco work (Ill. 58). He formed the hand-rail like a groove, as in the first Goetheanum.[15]

The same problems apply to the finalizing of the terrace structure with its balustrade profile, its piers,

entrances and windows. The masterly interpretation of Rudolf Steiner's sketches, which we have already discussed without attribution, we owe to the sculptor Oswald Dubach.

How much in architecture has to do with proportion is obvious from Dubach's varied treatment of the north and south entrances. Even in the seemingly strict symmetry of the building there can be detected a subtle asymmetry. Our sense of proportion tells us that the flanking piers in the north must be broader than those in the south. Moreover, the trapezium-shaped capping to the pillars shows a different, shallower slope. The openings at the entrance are not only longer but have straight tops as well, whereas those to the south are haunched (Figs. 47, 48).

The artistic path followed by both Dubach and Kemper led from their native Russia to Dornach, where they performed valuable service on the wooden building, before volunteering to serve in the First World War. Both returned to Dornach after the war to resume their artistic activities.

The grouping of the windows in the eastern wall of the stage block was finally carried out according to a sketch by the painter Henny Geck, after the architects had submitted various proposals.

In the section dealing with the original model, a table was introduced to simplify comparison between the first and the second design stages (see p. 50). For the sake of completeness it seems proper in a similar way to summarize the third stage of planning, according to which, though stretched over a longer period of time, the building was actually constructed.

Building application of April–May 1924	1924–8 finalized design
Terrace of the old building still included. Reaches only to the eastern limit of the wing extensions.	An encircling substructure suited to the new building, worked out on the basis of sketches.
Superstructure drawn according to the model.	Western part of the superstructure according to the model, but lowered by an average of 600 mm. Total width of the wings increased by 3 m.
Eastern section according to the model, without a terrace and extended down to the ground.	Eastern section modified according to sketches, adding corner pilasters and an architrave-like cornice around three sides of the roof. Raised in comparison to the model so that the step between the roof over the wings and that over the stage-block is abandoned (see drawing of 30 January 1925).
Window openings still tentative.	Window and door openings architecturally consistent.

Thus we may attribute to Rudolf Steiner himself the model, sketches showing the basic allocation of spaces, the additional design of the terrace and modified eastern block, as well as indications for certain window shapes. To his co-workers was left solely the interior planning and design of rooms and of window and door openings. Attention is called to this circumstance once again, since public opinion with regard to the second Goetheanum is subject to errors on this point that are still in circulation.

66

The Engineering Achievement

Rudolf Steiner had realized the importance of reinforced concrete at an early date, and it lay close to his heart to put this modern mouldable material to use in suitable building situations. This represented a welcome challenge for a young inventive technician like Ole Falk Ebbell.

Ebbell was born in 1879 in Trondheim, Norway. His career as a structural engineer began before the First World War with the Basel Building Society, where he made his first acquaintance with the special building tasks at the Goetheanum. He was involved in the construction of the double-domed building, also with the residences, and above all with the reinforced concrete building that housed the central heating plant. It was ten years later that, having meanwhile achieved an independent status as partner to Leuprecht in Basel, he was commissioned by the General Anthroposophical Society with the structural engineering work on the second Goetheanum.

The contract between the planning office at the Goetheanum and the civil engineers was signed on 20 November 1924. This was extended on 24 January 1925 to include greater responsibility on the site and defining this in relation to the architects' duties. Decades later Ebbell acknowledged, "As an engineer I was never granted such freedom as I enjoyed among the anthroposophists. It was *ideal* . . . !" Buoyed up by such trust, he and his colleagues were able to carry through a pioneer achievement, which even today arouses the admiration of experts.

For the tricky calculation work on the roof trusses they called on Ernst Suter, who had just returned to Switzerland and was strong on the mathematical side. It was no easy task, for not only were there three unknowns, but each truss was different.

Ebbell vividly recalled this planning period. "Steiner lay ill at the time. We had the architects' drawings and later the large model to 1:20 scale, to which we had to conform — Steiner was very exact — but no one interfered with our work." To describe the unusual problem of constructing the shell of the western staircase, he, the engineer, had recourse to a sculptural comparison. It was, he said, as if one had to be a Rodin, but must mould the surfaces from the inside. His aim was to make the freely modelled walls as thin as possible. And these skin walls between the bracing are indeed for the most part no more than 120–150 mm (5–6 inches) thick (Ills. 49, 56). The use of reinforced concrete, he explained, was still in its beginning stages. There was little experience to go by. With pride he mentioned his guiding principle: to use no more concrete than was absolutely necessary — no more than 16 litres of concrete for every cubic metre of building volume. That was not much, he thought, but he added that they had blundered as to water. Often the water was poured in by the bucket — 50 to 60 litres per cubic metre of concrete. He wanted to learn by experience on the spot, however. He stood next to the man at the mixing machine and sounded him out, for it was he who had discovered the mistake. After that, they made the concrete much drier — 40 litres of water per cubic metre. The strength of the concrete achieved in the construction of the Goetheanum has proven itself over the years.

From the admiring tone in a daily press account of a visit to the construction site by professionals, the quality of this engineering feat is apparent:

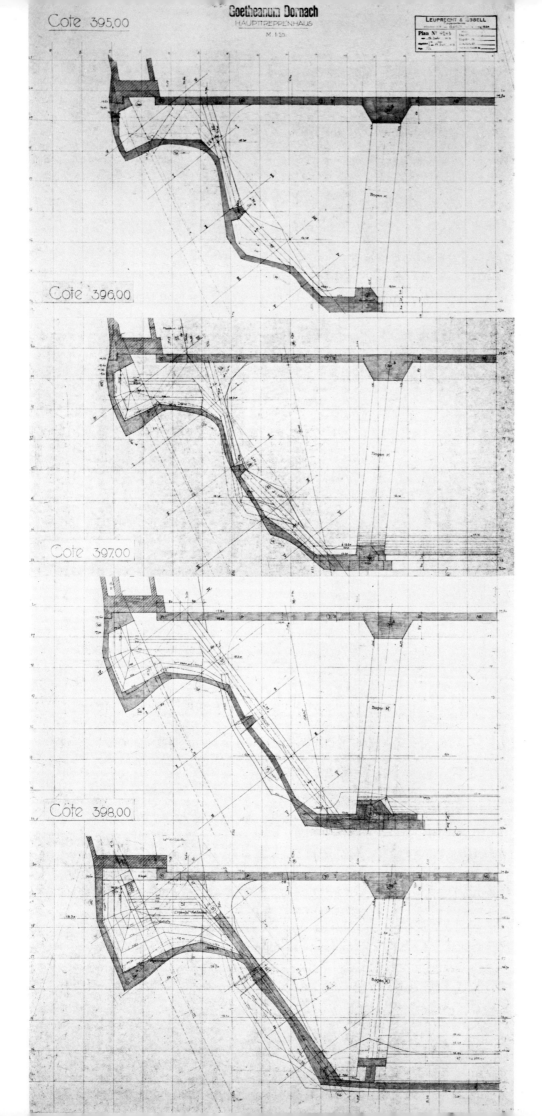

Cote 395,00

Goetheanum Dornach
HAUPTTREPPENHAUS
M. 1:20.

LEUPRECHT & EBBELL
Plan N° 42+3

Cote 396,00

Cote 397,00

Cote 398,00

49   From the structural engineers' drawings for the formwork. Upper part of western staircase: four contours at intervals of 1 m.

The Solothurn Daily (19 January 1927):
The Goetheanum in Dornach

"In the last few days the roof has been closed in over the two main sections – auditorium and stage block – now under construction in the new Goetheanum. Thereby a significant juncture in the construction of this impressively laid-out theatre building has been reached. As is well known, the entire building is to be carried out as a unified structure in reinforced concrete. It constitutes as to type and dimensions, large by our standards, one of the most interesting projects now being built in Switzerland. Technically, and particularly for the engineer, this building has posed difficult problems.

"Shortly before the new year, the Engineers and Architects Society of Solothurn visited the construction site. The present phase contains much of interest to the professional eye, such as cannot be seen later on. Thus several sections of most unusual and generous-sized scaffolding supporting the form-work could be inspected. Under the guidance of the client's representative, Mr. Ernst Aisenpreis, the architect-in-charge, supported by the engineer, Mr. Ebbell of the firm of Leuprecht and Ebbell, Basel, who has been entrusted with the reinforced concrete work, the building was inspected from top to bottom. Its significance can be gathered from a single figure, namely that about 15,000 cubic metres of reinforced concrete have been employed. For this no less than 1700 railway waggon loads of sand and gravel and 450 waggon loads of cement have been required. Impressive were the 30 metre framed trusses spanning the great hall and the reinforced concrete braced trusses over the 24 metre wide stage, which had to be supported with scaffolding 25 metres high.

"Following this highly interesting tour, the visitors took in the total architectural impression of the building. To be sure the scaffolding still stands, and the low-lying terrace structure is missing, which is to surround the entire building (but will not alter the general effect in any unfavourable way). None the less, one is already able to form a broad judgement. This is, that the building, despite its size, will fit relatively well into the landscape, and that the many, and most serious, doubts that have been expressed in this regard were without substance."

Although Ebbell's life brought him rich experience, many tasks in other directions and major responsibilities, in his clarified view back over half a century, it was precisely the Dornach period that occupied a central place in his consciousness. He died in Berne, where he had retired, in his ninety-first year.

Execution Under Direct Management
In building the first Goetheanum, the Basel Building Society or Construction Company was drawn in as contractor and engineering office. Not all the experience gathered at that time was satisfactory. In putting up the second Goetheanum it was decided that their own Planning and Management Office, which had existed from the beginning to handle certain of the building projects on the Dornach hill, should be expanded into a proper General Contracting Office. Thus the General Anthroposophical Society itself carried out to a certain extent the building of its own headquarters.

The necessary labourers, tradesmen and specialists were hired by its own management; the materials, equipment and machinery acquired or hired; the building site arrangements made and maintained. The inventories and books of that time reveal a situation of great interest both from a human and a management point of view. The number of those entering or leaving employment during the six years from 1924 to 1929 shows that the continuing level of skilled and un-skilled labourers during the building period at the Goetheanum lay on the average around a hundred.

The Building Operation at the Goetheanum: Employees

	Entering	Leaving	Personnel
1923	9	–	9
1924	159	67	101
1925	265	242	124
1926	84	121	87
1927	51	65	73
1928	80	35	118
1929	–	21	97
	648	551	

In 1930 a further relatively large number of workmen departed, for once again a construction period had come to an end.

A survey of the building trades represented by the hired labour makes it abundantly clear that this was a project done in reinforced concrete.

Of the total of 648 employees entered by name in this given period, no less than 129 were carpenters, 38 were joiners and 28 steel fixers. Next came 20 masons and plasterers and one each of the following: a contractor, a foreman, a concreter, a specialist in formwork and a blasting operator. In addition there were in all eleven electricians, plumbers, machinists, turners, locksmiths and mechanics, and five painters.

But the list is not yet complete. Besides these 237 skilled labourers, there were 377 unskilled labourers, workers employed by the week, handymen and one volunteer. The construction site on the hill must have been spick-and-span, to judge by the impressive army of 30 cleaning women, who in the course of these few years unfolded their invaluable activities. We recognize further from the list of personnel that the building management at the Goetheanum, beyond construction matters, had to concern itself with dramatic art and the new art of movement on the one hand and to foster a connection with the natural surroundings on the other. We find mentioned a laundress, a dyer, a seamstress, a gardening hand and three cherry pickers.

Judging by today's inflated standards, the hourly wages paid in those days are surprising. However, they were entirely in accordance with the current rate in that area.

Building Trade	Hourly Wage (in Swiss francs)
Joiner	1.30 to 2.20
Carpenter	2.00 to 2.88
Mason and Plasterer	1.50 to 1.90
Electrician, Plumber, Machinist, Turner	1.75 to 2.00
Mates or Labourers on weekly contract	0.70 to 0.90
Unskilled Labourers	1.25 to 1.48

In addition to this changing corps of workmen a hundred strong, it is necessary to consider the staff of professional architects, sculptors and office employees who were active in Dornach as members of the Anthroposophical Society. They devoted themselves wholeheartedly to fulfilling what were for them lofty goals and were satisfied with a very modest return.

If it is no longer possible to indicate the precise contribution of each of the persons whose name is given at the end of this book as being directly involved in work on the site, nevertheless the result of their efforts is a testimonial to its quality. Above all, the construction gave scope to and bears evidence of their devoted labour. The attitude that Rudolf Steiner himself fostered in such matters is revealed in a telling way in words spoken during the building of the first Goetheanum. This can equally well serve as an appreciation of what was done in the course of the work on its successor in reinforced concrete.

At an annual meeting on 21 October 1917 Steiner had said:

"I would like to make the suggestion that in the reports given at our general meetings, which will provide the basis for a chronicle of our building impulse, besides recognition for the flow of financial means and other matters, the names of our faithful co-workers should be mentioned, and in detail. Anyone who knows what an endless amount of work has been poured into the whole building activity, must feel it to be a self-evident duty to mention in such reports above all our faithful co-workers, with an indication of what they do. This could even be, in view of the present circumstances, of extraordinary importance and significance, quite apart from the fact that an objective report would, as I believe, pay its debt of gratitude thereby to those who have contributed such a quantity and fulness of work towards completion of the sculptural 'group' and of our building. It cannot in fact be measured nor highly enough prized."[16]

The expression "in view of the present circumstances", implies that the First World War was then raging. There was always the possibility that many who had played their part in the building would never return. Thus it was appropriate that their accomplishment be given its due, not only for the present but for the future as well. Whoever is concerned to transmit the historic facts about the building on the Dornach hill, will know their value, especially when he perceives to what a degree it lived in the consciousness of the builder of the Goetheanum. "How great are the obstacles for future annalists, how difficult it is to dig out many of the facts, to get the history straight."[16]

One fact, however, can be set down with absolute certainty and the fullest conviction: not only the domed building, but also its concrete successor, if it was to arise at all, had need of an untiring contribution from people who had recognized the necessity for a free spiritual life and were therefore prepared to cope with a "free" economic situation.

Due to increasing building costs, as well as to the novelty and magnitude of the building project, it was apparent at the inception of work that the means furnished by the insurance would not cover the costs of a reinforced concrete shell according to the model, to say nothing of completing the extensive interior. From an illustrated supplement to the news bulletin No. 30 for members of the Anthroposophical Society, entitled *Demolition and Reconstruction in Dornach*, we learn of the creative way in which the original Executive Council (Vorstand), four months after the death of Rudolf Steiner, made an appeal for funds to the friends of the building. (See the translation of the Appeal on p. 73.)

The suggestion met with enthusiastic response from all sides. On 1 November 1925 it was possible to announce that people in various countries in a spirit of personal sacrifice had promised to provide the following:

Switzerland	Windows and doors (which gave access to the landscape of the homeland)
Germany	The stage
England	Lighting
Holland	Heating; floor and wall covering

France ⎫
Italy ⎬ Stage curtains
Belgium ⎭

Austria ⎫
Poland ⎬ Auditorium seats
Czechoslovakia ⎭

Finland ⎫
Esthonia ⎬ Completion of the stairways

Norway ⎫
Sweden ⎬ The slate roof
Denmark ⎭

America   Terrace and ventilation
Honolulu   Initial interior decoration

The Treasurer

The sum anticipated from the fire insurance company amounted to 3,183,000 Swiss francs, according to a memorandum of the Cantonal Treasury in Solothurn, dated 11 June 1923. Thus the aim was now to raise a further $1\frac{1}{2}$ million francs through donations. This would cover the cost of completing the parts just mentioned. In this way it would be possible to erect the entire shell and to finish and equip enough of it to start using the building, even if it remained incomplete. But would things go according to plan? Would the inflationary tendencies continue and prices continue to rise? Could one count on all the promised gifts?

Dr Günther Wachsmuth, the secretary and treasurer of the world-wide society centred at the Goetheanum, felt this situation to be a challenge never to tire in his efforts to raise the necessary funds. Now and up to the time of his death in the spring of 1963, he could hear the words of Rudolf Steiner resounding in his ears: it was an ''iron necessity'' to put up the new Goetheanum. Wachsmuth was a scientist. It would be

the task of a special essay to do justice to his scientific achievements – for example, his research into rhythms. The historian of the Goetheanum, gaining insight into his many-sided activities, must marvel at the way this tireless servant of the cause for which he laboured, beyond the discharge of his other duties, could make such demands on himself for the sake of the building. It is not too much to say that it is thanks to him the Goetheanum did not remain a torso without a face. His efforts created the west front.

He faced the essentials squarely. All of his qualities – his cosmopolitan interests and knowledge, his capacity for enthusiasm, his loyalty, his characteristic quick-footedness, his lively manner of presenting facts – all were concentrated on the attainment of his goal. The means did not flow in at a pace to match the construction. The tempo at the building site had to be slowed down. As the table (p. 70) indicates, during 1926 and 1927 fewer workers were hired, many left and the balance of workmen declined. This was the signal for the treasurer to intensify his efforts and to inspire all active helpers. Günther Wachsmuth took to the road. The versatile Dutch artist, Jan Stuten, who had a part in the interior design of the new building, accompanied him. Starting in 1926, they held lantern lectures about the Goetheanum and the impulse behind it, how it had achieved a comprehensive expression in the first building and how it was once again in process of being realized in the new building. Lectures were given in numerous cities of central, northern, eastern and western Europe. In a report on the opening of the Rudolf Steiner Hall in London, 1–6 June 1926, Albert Steffen recorded: ''On the 5th Dr. Guenther Wachsmuth roused enthusiasm with his lecture on the Dornach architecture, whilst Jan Stuten spoke on the interior design for the Goetheanum. The desire soon to have a home in Dornach worthy of

Dear Friends!

Whatever we do as anthroposophists stands within the larger historic perspective of past, present and future. In the last year of his life our teacher made this clear to us in his lectures on karma.

Our brothers of the past, and we ourselves, experienced in medieval times how splendid buildings that served as centres for spiritual training were destroyed by fire. Forces of mighty communal enthusiasm built up again what had been destroyed. Let us recall what lived in our brothers of the past, e.g. at Chartres. "In the night of 7 to 8 September of the year 1020, that is on the night before the Festival of the Birth of the Virgin Mary, which under Fulbert had become so important precisely in Chartres, the venerable church fell victim to the flames. Forthwith Fulbertus took up the rebuilding of the church with energy. Despite the greatest personal sacrifice, made by himself, his clerics and by many others, to consummate the rebuilding of the church 'with unheard-of splendour', the task exceeded by far the local sources of help. Fulbertus turned therefore to the numerous lands of Europe, entreating financial aid, and so great indeed was his personal authority and also the especial veneration which all peoples held for the seat at Chartres, that means flowed in in sufficient measure, even from Canute the Great, King of Denmark and England. The church was rebuilt on the same spot, upon the hill where once, according to tradition, the sacred grove of the Druids had stood."

Magnificent are the ancient accounts that show us how building was done in the twelfth and thirteenth centuries. What a spirit took hold of whole populations! Listen to a letter from Hugo of Amiens from the year 1145. "In Chartres the people, seized by a spirit of humility, hauled carts and waggons, in order to be of help in the building of the cathedral. Reports of this spread far and wide and enflamed the inhabitants of Normandy as well to emulate the piety of their neighbours. The believers from our province went first to Chartres to render the tribute of their offerings to the Mother of God. They constitute holy brotherhoods, to which no one is admitted who does not confess his errors and make peace with his enemies. The brothers choose a leader, at whose call they all, in obedience and piety, bring together their offerings in carts. The abbot Haymond writes in those same days that the pious custom of joining together in order to work on the cathedrals had its beginning at Chartres. From there it was said to have spread to Normandy and other lands. It was a noble enthusiasm that gripped all classes of society. Men and women, rich and poor, spanned themselves to the waggons on which they hauled lime, stones, wood and food for the workmen. The loads were enormous; often the exertions of a thousand pilgrims were needed to get a single waggon going. At the word of the priests all feelings of hatred were assuaged and a noble harmony arose in their hearts. If some stubborn sinner refused to forgive his enemies, he was driven away in shame and disgrace, and the offering he had loaded on to his waggon was refused. Arrived at the goal of their journey, the pilgrims lined up their waggons in rows about the church and set up a kind of camp in which they spent the night in prayer." Thus was Chartres built up again in the shortest time.

Our brothers in the future, at the end of the twentieth century, and we ourselves, are to bring together again Platonism and Aristotelianism in independent universities. These friends of ours at the end of the century will have much to say about what we are now doing. For we are now to lay the spiritual and physical foundation-stone for their work. So do we Anthroposophists go to work in the present, drawing our impulses from the past and being observed from the future.

We, the brothers of the present, must build up again with the enthusiasm of our friends of the twelfth and thirteenth centuries, and with our eyes turned towards what the end of the century is expecting of us, and according to which it will judge us.

The only sounds from the outer world that penetrated to the sickbed of our leader during the last days of his life were the sawing and hammering on the building site of the Goetheanum. He loved this noise and enquired every day how the new building was progressing, gave advice, corrected drawings, spurred on the work. Of this we may be sure: he expects us to carry out this building from the model that he loved, to the end that the spiritual foundation stone which he laid in our hearts at Christmas 1923 may strengthen and enspirit us to raise the centre for the teaching of his 'Anthroposophy' over the physical foundation stone which he himself laid and which still stands.

Anthroposophy teaches us, to be sure, that we in the twentieth century cannot help in the same way as did our brothers in the thirteenth century. But every anthroposophist can help, in the twentieth century, with the sacrifice that overcomes Ahriman.

The suggestion of the Executive Council would be, that those elements of the interior of the building, which will still be missing when the building has been erected, be apportioned to individual countries in such a way that one country would accept the task of underwriting the stage equipment, another provide the means for the windows, another for the seating, still another for heating and lighting, for the curtain, for the organ, etc. In this way every country in which anthroposophists live today would contribute its part to the common building. A building such as this would become unique on earth through this simple fact.

The new Goetheanum, for which our leader bequeathed us the model, and whose realization has become our sacred task, if it is erected out of the common labour of anthroposophists over the entire earth, will be worthy of our past and a good and firm foundation for our brothers in the future.

The building is a world-historic necessity. We cordially invite all anthroposophists to help us.

The Executive Council
of the General Anthroposophical Society:
Albert Steffen.   Marie Steiner.   Dr. Ita Wegman.
Dr. E. Vreede.   Dr. Guenther Wachsmuth.

Anthroposophy was alive among all those present, not only the Dornachers."

Between 22 May and 9 November 1927, the two men were in Hamburg, Oslo, Stockholm, Breslau, Berlin, Danzig, Cologne, Karlsruhe, Pforzheim, Mannheim, Stuttgart, Vienna, Prague, London and The Hague. To begin with, the artistic achievement was allowed to speak for itself. Then the financial picture was analysed. "The living quality of Dr. Wachsmuth's presentation", so went a contemporary report, "made it possible to follow what he had to say from beginning to end with inner engagement, to live into the various stages of the construction of the new building, which one could follow up to the removal of the formwork from the concrete, the taking down of the scaffolding and finally to the emergence of this mighty edifice in its natural setting."[17]

Neither he nor the others at the scene of building activity relaxed in their efforts. At his side stood above all Albert Steffen with advice and encouragement. A year after the appeal of July 1925, to which we have already alluded, the Dornach Executive Committee issued a new illustrated letter in July 1926. Such an appeal needs to be studied in detail in order to appreciate its distinctive tone, persuasive yet at the same time leaving the reader free. Each succeeding appeal sounded a new note. Shortly before Michaelmas, in anticipation of the topping out ceremony, Steffen reported on a visit of the President of the Swiss Confederation to the growing structure and then exclaimed: "Without a building the Anthroposophical Society remains homeless." At Easter 1927 a new appeal went out to the world. Of the goal that had finally been set of nearly two million francs, hardly half had come in. Such was the circumstance that led to the treasurer's personal campaign. At that time it was still hoped to dedicate the building to its use in the spring of 1928.

But since the topping out did not take place until Michaelmas 1926 and the wooden statue was not transferred to the eastern part of the unfinished building before Michaelmas 1927, the opening of the building could not be foreseen earlier than Michaelmas 1928. This date was made public on 27 May 1928. Only 89,000 francs were then lacking to reach the financial goal. Photographs that accompanied the announcement showed the entire building with its modelled western part and its terrace freed of scaffolding. The campaign had been a success. The building had a "face" and looked out into the world towards the west.

On the 1 July 1928, Wachsmuth was able to report that thousands of interested people were asking to be shown through the still unfinished building. On Whit Sunday there had been more than a thousand visitors on a single afternoon. Hardly a week went by without some organization, whether of a scientific, technical, artistic or social nature, requesting a tour. Not only in the local press but also in distant countries this unusual building achievement roused an astonished, often admiring, occasionally understanding echo.

The whole phenomenon is an example prompting earnest reflection on the evolutionary curve of the twentieth century. The interest that first showed itself seemed to be engulfed in an oppressive cloud between the years 1928 and 1960. Though it was much visited, it was little understood. The rediscovery of the Goetheanum after an interim of over thirty years has been reported in the introductory chapter.

After such a strenuous prelude, it is understandable that the opening ceremony took place in a similar mood. All the active participants were challenged to contribute to the conference only what was new in the development of their scientific or artistic fields.

Illustrations on pages 76 and 77

51   Timber formwork with steel reinforcement in the western roof area before concreting. 30. 9. 1926.

52   Timber formwork with steel reinforcement in the western roof area before concreting.

The contributions matched this challenge. Weeks in advance all the available quarters in the neighbourhood had been booked up. The reservation of rooms extended as far as Basel. Nevertheless, despite the absolute maximum number of guests, every member who had applied in time was guaranteed admission and lodgings. Reporting on the conference, the president, Albert Steffen, was able to write: "Our long-cherished expectations have been fulfilled. The Goetheanum has established itself as the bearer of spiritual impulses. Tireless effort and conscientious performance have been evidenced on all sides, even culminating in some creative achievements of an impressive kind. Even the mistakes that were made have proved fruitful.

"Widely travelled participants in the conference are justified in asking: Where else can one see and hear such things? Where else do men enter so whole-heartedly into what they do? Where else are such possibilities to be found?"[18]

However, Albert Steffen did not neglect to draw attention to the conditions that would have to be satisfied if such possibilities were to bear further fruit.

Thus did the new Goetheanum, raised in concrete, show itself to be not only a rock, but also a well-spring in a time of drought. And it is only because of its continued striving for freedom in science and art that it has been possible to sketch the *Future Prospect*, which form our concluding chapter.

The Administration of the Goetheanum Building

Characteristic of the realism of the creator of the Goetheanum is the manner in which the existing Goetheanum Association was reorganized at the founding of the General Anthroposophical Society. The building was given its own administration, forming one of the four departments of the Society. For its administrative tasks it was even provided with its own letterhead designed by Rudolf Steiner himself. The responsibilities of the Association that had to do specifically with the building, its personnel and upkeep were taken over by the Administration of the Goetheanum Building. The Architects' Office then formed one of its sub-sections.

The architect-in-charge, Ernst Aisenpreis, was declared the first technical head of this Administration. Associates who joined it shortly after its formation – Elsy Ruschmann and Emil Estermann – were then in a position after his death in 1949 to assume the administrative side of his responsibility.

Estermann confirms that the cost of the building, including its partial equipping and furnishing up to the end of 1929, amounted to 4,765,491.90 Swiss francs. Bearing in mind the volume of over 110,000 cubic metres, this sum implies a provisional cubic metre price of 43 francs. By 31 December 1934, building costs had meanwhile reached the sum of 5,188,437.48 Swiss francs. However, the political events of this period signified the drying up of one of the chief sources of gift money for the building, namely Germany. Thus, much had to remain unfinished. The work on the interior had to wait nearly twenty years before it could be taken up again. Then, in 1952, the smaller auditorium with stage at ground level – the so-called "Foundation Stone Hall" (Grundstein-Saal) – and, in 1956, the interior of the great hall was completed. Further parts were brought to completion in the ensuing years, up to the recent past. But still there are unfinished rooms.

53   The Goetheanum under construction. View from the south. Whitsun 1926.

54   The Goetheanum under construction. View from the west. Easter 1927. This was the stage reached when Le Corbusier made his first visit.

The Right Man in the Right Place

When the time is ripe for something new and significant, the best of ideas and intentions are not enough. The right man must be at hand for each stage of its execution. The Goetheanum was no exception. This was forced on Aisenpreis' attention most clearly at the moment when the model of the artist-architect and the structural engineer's plans for the reinforcement and formwork had to be translated literally into "concrete reality". The carpentry work involved in building up the wooden shuttering demanded a capacity of spatial visualization far above the ordinary. The matrices had of course to be the exact negative of the desired building forms. The fact that they had been modelled, drawn and calculated by no means insured that they could be carried out. For this, the right man had to be found. At this juncture Aisenpreis called to mind the foreman of the carpentry shop, Heinrich Liedvogel, the master craftsman who had come to Dornach thirteen years before from Heidelberg and had done yeoman service in erecting the wooden building and its ancillary structures. "When the building is finished, Liedvogel, you and I will design furniture together," Steiner once promised him while the construction was going on. In his later years the master joiner remarked rather sadly, as if life had denied him something, that this had never been fulfilled.

This highly qualified craftsman was summoned by the chief architect and questioned whether he felt capable of preparing the wooden forms for the most difficult, freely-modelled parts of the exterior walling. As the two men looked at each other for a moment in silence, Aisenpreis was unsure whether the master joiner would be willing to undertake a carpenter's task. But Liedvogel had another question: Were there drawings he could take home with him? He wanted to study them before giving an answer. This he did until the small hours. The next day he explained to Aisenpreis how he would tackle the problem. The formwork would have to be made in large sections in the workshop, where there would be points and planes of reference. Then these sections would need to be carried by crane to their appointed positions and braced for the pouring of the concrete.

The achievement of Heinrich Liedvogel and his assistants has often been acknowledged, and rightly so. Such tributes can be underlined here by pointing to the book *Building in Visual Concrete* (London 1967). Of all the buildings shown, the only example of wooden formwork is that of the strongly overhanging roof of the Goetheanum. When one takes into account the appropriateness of concrete as a material for achieving the sculptural qualities of concavity and convexity, then one is in a position to assess the importance of the formwork in the negative as that which makes the poured form a positive reality (Ills. 51, 52).

Although Rudolf Steiner had had the concrete used in his first Goetheanum worked over sculpturally after it had set, here the possibility was present of winning the forms directly from the pouring process. This proved feasible through the expert collaboration of artists, architects and craftsmen. It was they who made his architectural inheritance accessible to posterity in the form of this monolithic structure in concrete. When it was finally disencumbered of its scaffolding in the spring of 1928, it could at last reveal its impressive contours unhindered.

The planning of architects and technicians alike for the interior had of necessity to be done rather more independently and gropingly, for here there were no sketches by Steiner, but only scanty indications to go by. His drawings for the interior were schematic to the highest degree, and in the plans prepared for the

Illustrations on pages 82 and 83

56   The western staircase under construction. 23. 1. 1928.

57   The western staircase after provisional glazing. 16. 11. 1928.

55   The Goetheanum freed of its scaffolding. 23. 9. 1928.

58 The staircase in the south wing under construction. 16. 11. 1928.

59 The western staircase at first floor level.

preliminary application it is hard to judge where his direct influence is to be traced. As has already been said, he put his signature to these plans at once, clearly in order to speed things up and certainly counting on opportunities to guide developments as the work proceeded. It was also his intention to make a model for the interior. The more one studies the exterior model, the more one recognizes that the forms visible on the outside presuppose and reflect an interior plan; a clear disposition of functions.

Form, Colour, Light, Word

Standing inside the western staircase and studying its construction, we can observe how the exterior forms work in with such effect that it seems we are moving about inside a giant sculpture. Perhaps this fact will explain why smaller, subordinate sculptural motifs, so prominent in the first building, could be totally excluded here. This is particularly evident where the interior design, as originally conceived by architects and other artists at the time, could not be fully carried out because of lack of funds. Perhaps this has brought about something closer to what Steiner had intended — a direct interpretation and utterly simple execution. The outline of the constructional and bracing elements now to be seen in the central and upper parts of the staircase can only be understood in terms of the stucco work envisaged in a model by Jan Stuten but not carried out.

In the western staircase, which, as it now stands, has been worked over less than the stairway to the south, we experience strongly to what an extent the conditions of light have been taken into consideration. As we pass through the main entrance at ground level, we arrive first in a hall that is only scantily lit by daylight. This gives direct access to a cloakroom and circulation area. However, a bright light streams towards us from the sides, down the two broad flights of stairs, and climbing them we arrive at an intermediate storey which is strongly illumined by daylight. The stairways here appear to open into a wide space — an impression brought about by the changed condition of light. From here we can reach the terrace, which affords us a view of the landscape on all sides. The glazing of the central rectangular opening in the west, 8 m in width by almost 7 m in height, presented a problem that was solved by Hermann Ranzenberger in metal. Further steps to left and right lead us upward again into a darker region. Here we arrive at a landing where both flights unite. A final short broad flight of steps then leads us up to the three double doors in the west that open into the main auditorium. This landing area is dominated by subdued coloured light issuing from an expanse of red glass — the upper west window. In executing this red window, the same glass engraving technique was used as in the corresponding window of the first Goetheanum. The colour is also the same. This is true of the windows in the great hall as well, whose colours and themes are derived from the first building. The forms of the window openings, however, have a different character in the second Goetheanum. The decision to use Steiner's earlier designs for the etching of the new glass windows was apparently still made during his lifetime. Responsibility for this work was entrusted to Assya Turgenieff. She has bequeathed to posterity a valuable account of her experiences over many years in this field.[19]

The colour that floods through a space is for Steiner one of its more important aspects, whether it has its source, as here, in coloured windows, or in painted walls. What he worked to achieve was a wall colour treatment that tended, through the quality of the colour

62   *The stage extension to the south.*

Illustrations on pages 90 and 91

63   *North side from the west.*

64   *Detail of the western staircase at terrace level.*

itself, to render the walls transparent, or, as he expressed it himself in 1923, "To free colour from gravity, to experience colour as an independent element, to make colours eloquent."[20]

The technique that was to make such an effect possible he found in transparent veil painting, using thin layers of colour or glazes. Ever since the building of the Stuttgart centre for the Anthroposophical Society in 1911, this problem had been worked on more intensively, in order to lend the walls a weightless colour quality. Thus the thought of transparent colour in space had emerged in all its significance before the buildings in Dornach were begun. In the year 1911 in Stuttgart it was said, "We shall make the significance of the various shades of colour most clear to our souls, if we describe their effect on the occultist. It is necessary for him to detach himself from everything else and give himself up completely to the given shade of colour, dissolving into it. As he surrenders himself to the colour covering physically opaque walls, and should he be in certain respects advanced as an occult student, then, after a time of such complete surrender, it would come about that the walls disappear from his clairvoyant view. The consciousness is no longer cut off from the surrounding world by walls. It is not as though he sees the neighbouring houses outside, or as if the walls were made of glass. Rather it is that the circumference opens up to reveal a world of phenomena of a purely spiritual kind. A series of spiritual facts and beings become visible."[21]

The colour treatment described here and the resulting experience of colour can in some cases be more important for the interior decorator than the material of the enclosing walls. In the second Goetheanum, Rudolf Steiner wanted the element of colour, as well as the pictorial element, to take precedence over the sculptural. As early as the year 1923 two artists were encouraged to concern themselves with the problem of a ceiling painting for the great hall of the future Goetheanum. This project still awaits its realization. The cupola paintings of the first Goetheanum were executed in plant colours. This is an area still at the experimental stage. Its importance, however, is not to be underestimated. In the autumn of 1971 it was possible to decorate an entire ground floor lecture hall in this manner, using transparent layers of plant colour.

Contrasting with this element of colour, which maintains its original character in the second building, is the sculptural element. In Rudolf Steiner's later, mature building, we see the richly alternating play of concave and convex forms unfolding in simple, expressive surfaces that now have taken on more of an angular character. His command of the doubly-bent surface produces here the "semblance of life". It is not difficult to picture such a surface in theory; it can be calculated mathematically and is applied to many everyday objects in a more or less unconscious way. We see it most clearly, perhaps, in a saddle; more familiarly, if less obviously, in a jug or bottle at the juncture of belly and neck. Steiner observed that such tendencies are present everywhere in the organic world. He saw, for instance, a particular inspiration for the architectural artist in the forms of bones and the skeleton. He arrived at his knowledge of form from such organic shapes, making use of Goethe's scientific observations and leading on to various applications of this fundamental sculptural theme. From this arises the play of elevations and depressions to which every artist working in a sculptural medium must devote himself wittingly or unwittingly. Starting as a scientist, Steiner moved on into the artistic field and there made a discovery which with most artists remains in the unconscious. Only out of this kind of artistic effort have

66, 67, 68   *Window detail.*

72   *Contour of the southern wing from the east.*

73   *Column and projecting western staircase to the south.*

74   *South-eastern corner pilaster from the south.*

76–80 *Buttress details of the south wing.*

81   Upper part of west front from the north-west.

82   Detail of west front, north side. View from below.

83   Detail of west front from the north-west.

the forms in a building such as the second Goetheanum become "eloquent".

In the case of the concrete building, the sculptural element holds sway chiefly in the exterior, whereas in the wooden building it found its main expression in the interior. This explains why from far and near the present building reveals so many aspects.

In dealing with the shape of the terrace on plan, it was said this was determined primarily by circles circumscribing both the substructure and the superstructure. Were the plan dominated by the concentric principle alone, it would be rigid and above all under the spell of a self-centred, "egoistic" principle. It is of decisive importance, therefore, that two sections of the building in the west — the protruding sculpturally treated staircase above, the projecting main entrance below — break through the charmed circle, grow out of it, one might even say actively push their way through it (e).

In attempting to substantiate this, the attentive

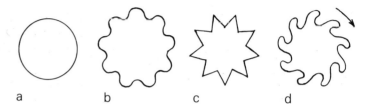

a   b   c   d

observer learns to grasp one of the central features of the organically living style of architecture. A simple exercise will demonstrate this. The architect's attention is drawn to a series of shapes derived from the circle.[22] In face of the plain circle a person sensitive to form will feel that he is placed on his own resources, resting within himself (a). To begin with this unarticulated line allows of two characteristic tendencies. In the first of these, rounded protrusions appear in the form of a wavy line (b), proclaiming the "victory from within". In the other, a zigzag line indicates that external forces have won the ascendancy (c). To round out the picture, attention is drawn to a third, less elementary development in this series, in which the wavy movement shows a definite direction (d). The experience we are discussing can be induced by a mere fragment of one of these forms (e).

As can be understood from Rudolf Steiner's statements and also from the building itself, its outer aspect is not derived from mere aesthetic theory. The exterior columns and corner pilasters, which express the supporting principle through root-like terminations below and a powerful expansion above, have arisen out of artistic necessity, just like the form of the building as a whole. This is why the building and its exterior forms do not leave the passer-by cold. We feel obliged to come to an understanding with it. And when we do this, we experience how the constructional and artistic elements are so closely entwined that they are no longer to be distinguished. Through Rudolf Steiner's way of working, the forces of weight and support

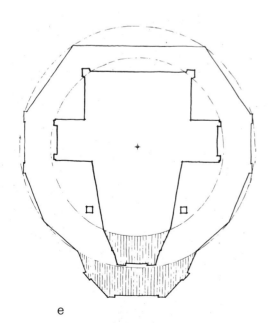

e

become a visible artistic synthesis. They attain a higher and more inward dignity by being appealed to as artistic and immaterial factors.

The sentiments aroused among lovers of architecture by this building thus do not lead to long-winded statements on aesthetic laws and the like. They lie much more immediately within the sense experience, and this is not to be conveyed in concepts. Is not this the reason why Corbusier exclaimed repeatedly, "Oh, la, la!", when he was shown through the half-finished building in 1927? Similarly, in July of 1963, while making a round of the terrace, the Japanese architect, Kenji Imai, paused musingly before one of the modelled window openings to the western staircase, felt with his sensitive hand the subtly rounded contours of its lower surfaces and gave vent to his feelings with a half-sung "M-m-m!" Gripped in his turn by a contemplation of the building, the American poet and dramatist Percy MacKaye gave eloquent expression to his discerning views in a sonnet.[23] For students of the German language — which Coleridge called "the modern Greek" — and as a monument to the friendship between the two poets, we append also Albert Steffen's convincing rendering of MacKaye's verse.

TO THE GOETHEANUM
Seen from Unterer Zielweg

Calm, silent thunder of the soul of things!
Vast immanence of passionate thought, made free
In archetypal purpose! Solemnly
As dawn your plastic spirit floats, and flings
The curved escarpments of your massive wings
To nestle the offspring of Immensity
In the human mind: Prescience of life to be:
Reverence of man for God's imaginings.

His brow from whom you sprang through Phoenix-fire
Here broods alike on April cherry-bloom
And autumn storm from your deep-sunken eyes,
Himself your silent thunder and your choir
Of sacred dawn. Above his quickening tomb
You lift the stature of his sacrifice.

Percy MacKaye

DAS GOETHEANUM
Vom unteren Zielweg gesehen

Ruhsam verhaltner Donnerton der Dinge!
Urgrund des Alls: – Idee! O Schöpferspiel
des freien Geistes, archetypisch Ziel!
Wie Morgendämmerung die Sonnenschwinge
entfaltet, dass als Laut das Licht erklinge,
gebogne Abdachung, massiver Kiel
umhüllt des Himmelskindes Stirnprofil.
Ehrfurcht in Gottes Bilderschaffen dringe!

Baumeisters Braue, Form aus Phönix-Feuer,
sinnt im April hoch über Kirschbaumblühen,
senkt sich im Herbststurm erdentief hinab.
Er selber ist der Donner, ungeheuer,
der schweigend winkt, Verkünder eines frühen
und heiligen Opferkeimes aus dem Grab.

Translated by Albert Steffen

86   The Goetheanum from the north. In the foreground the "Heizhaus", the "Verlagshaus" and a cupola of the "Glashaus".

Illustration on page 108
87   Site plan of the Dornach hill.

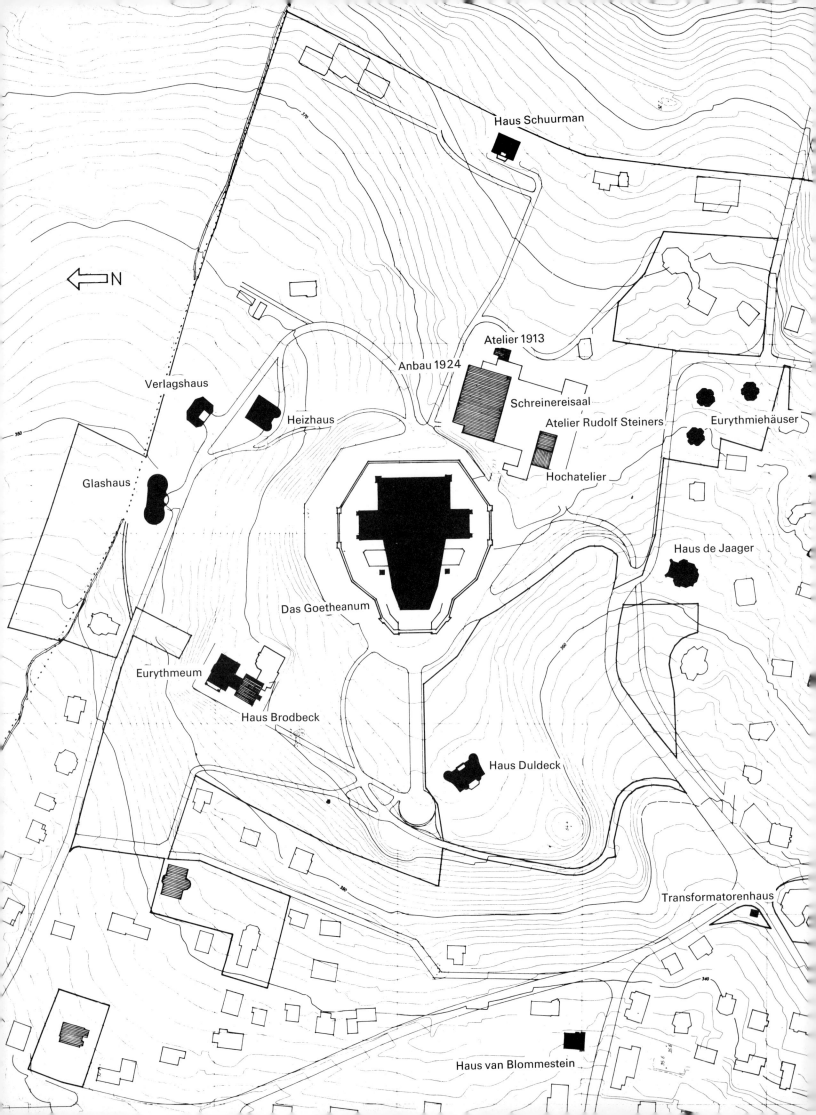

N

Haus Schuurman

Atelier 1913

Anbau 1924

Schreinereisaal

Verlagshaus

Atelier Rudolf Steiners

Eurythmiehäuser

Heizhaus

Hochatelier

Glashaus

Haus de Jaager

Das Goetheanum

Eurythmeum

Haus Brodbeck

Haus Duldeck

Transformatorenhaus

Haus van Blommestein

THE DORNACH HILL

The "Ridges of the Crags"

No one has described the quality of the Jura landscape south of Basel more beautifully than Goethe. He recorded the impressions afforded by a ride from this city on the Rhine to Bienne in one of his *Letters from Switzerland,*[24] which begins: "Since time immemorial the Birs, a modest river, has sought its way through the backbone of a lofty and broad mountain chain." His description of the landscape gains in intensity until it is almost as if a powerful architectural experience is being evoked: "Now a series of connecting walls rises perpendicularly, now mighty strata sweep steeply towards the river and the road. Broad masses are piled up one on the other and nearby cliffs drop abruptly downwards. Fissures cleave open, tearing massive slabs from the remaining rock. Isolated fragments of stone have toppled down, others still hang over precariously as if they too might fall in days to come.

"Blunt, pointed, overgrown, bare, the ridges of these crags rise above the others as single crests, bald and bold, whilst weathered crevices press against the wall faces and into the depths. The sublime affords the soul a grand repose; it is filled wholly with this and feels itself as large as it can ever be. . ."

It is as if "from time immemorial" the cradle for a "Goetheanum" had been prepared by Nature herself. Conversely, this work of architecture is able to translate the formative forces of nature, expressed here in limestone, as a corresponding human response for all men to interpret.

The relationship between these architectural forms and their surrounding world of rock and cliff is evident. This building truly belongs in its natural surroundings; it grows convincingly out of the place where it stands and interprets this milieu. But it does more. It seems to overcome what is lifeless, to incorporate something of the buoyancy of the world of trees as a sort of circulation. It reaches beyond itself and allows the changing atmosphere along with the creatures who live in the air to approach it. It must be seen to be believed how swallows and other birds fly in swarms from the west towards the modelled face of the projecting front, and then, as if in play, halt just short of the concrete wall, execute a reverse turn in full flight, only to repeat the same tactics again and again. In such movements the observer might perceive how the sculpting activity of the designer as he created his model is now, on a gigantic scale, executed as movement in the air.

Such atmospheric currents thus brought to visibility can be further refined and sublimated by the influence of light. Georg Hartmann, formerly a student of Oskar Schlemmer at the "Bauhaus" in Dessau, who switched from designing to teaching and has been director of the Pedagogical Seminar at the Goetheanum, depicts these light effects in a delicate word-painting:

"The student who daily makes his way to the Goetheanum sees this building at every time of day, at every season of the year, in an ever-changing aspect. Whether the building rears on some misty autumn morning, as if shrouded, into the slowly brightening blue of heaven; whether in winter the living forms of the roof are decked with snow; whether the Christmas sun at midday illumines the whole building from the south in shadowless light; whether at midsummer the same southern aspect is incised with mighty shadows thrown by the overhanging roof; whether misting rain or storm clouds alter the forms of the building, or on a summer afternoon a rainbow arches its glowing shape against the dark sky in the east; whether at midnight under a full moon the building looks like ivory against the starry heavens; or whether the evening glow after sunset causes the forms of this building to light up again in soft colours — each moment the Goetheanum is something new, something living, a being who reveals the life of its soul through its forms."[25]

Whoever visits the Goetheanum today soon recognizes that he has before him not merely an isolated building of unusual design. As soon as he nears this structure on its elevated site, the customary Swiss residences on the lower slopes seem to make way for an edifice which strongly differs from conventional domestic architecture. Here a house has been adapted to this particular design more or less successfully, here we see one which has obviously been executed by Rudolf Steiner himself. At last we arrive at the magnificent slope from which the main building towers. And yet this structure does not overpower its surroundings. Despite its size it is only partially visible above trees and houses. If the visitor is to appreciate the building as a whole, he must find a good vantage point some distance away — perhaps on the bank of the Birs in Aesch — or he must stand in immediate proximity. In the shadow of this great building, he is then able to survey the surrounding houses designed by Rudolf Steiner, which form as it were the kernel of all the structures on the hill.

The Dornach hill had already gained prominence in the Middle Ages. Here a decisive battle for Swiss independence was fought against the German feudal lords in the year 1499. To commemorate this date, a pathway leading up the hill from Dornach-Brugg was still called "Bluthügelweg" or Blood Hill Way in the thirties. Today it is simply called "Hügelweg" or Hill Way. The projecting building site does not lie on the ridge of the Jura. Above it thrones the ruin of Dorneck Castle which dominated the region in the Middle Ages. Higher still rise the cliffs of the Gempen, with their characteristic abruptly-falling contour.

If we approach the Goetheanum along the Hügelweg, architectural impressions fairly cascade upon us. At a glance we perceive the upward-thrusting chimney of the "Heizhaus" (central heating plant), the slate-covered cupolas of the "Glashaus" (glass engraving studio), the simple entrance front of the "Verlagshaus" (publishers' house) and the pillars and roof-forms of the "Eurythmeum" (eurythmy school). Behind and above them all tower the bold yet solemn contours of the Goetheanum. If we proceed past these ancillary buildings, the main structure seems itself to move and elevate its organic forms.

However, if we walk up the hill from the village along the steeply rising Herzentalstrasse, one small residence with a greenish slate roof is conspicuous amongst the conventional forms of the lower-lying houses and on closer scrutiny reveals the hand of Rudolf Steiner. This residence was built in 1920 for the Dutch painter Louise van Blommestein. Somewhat higher the little transformer house is sited, which Steiner designed in cubic forms. Climbing still higher we approach the Goetheanum from the south-west and see in a loose sequence the studio, "Haus de Jaager", the three "Eurythmiehäuser" (eurythmists' houses) and, at a certain distance to the east of the Goetheanum, "Haus Schuurman".

Saliently placed in this area is a simple, straggling timber structure — the carpenter's shop or "Schreinerei". This had in part been erected as early as 1913 as a provisional "builder's hut" for the first

Goetheanum. Additions continued to be made until the summer of 1924. Rudolf Steiner's own studio is also situated here, as well as the "tall studio" or "Hochatelier" where the model for the 9 m high wooden sculptural group, now standing in the Goetheanum, was worked out to full scale.

We can also reach the Goetheanum from the west along the "Philosopher's Walk" or "Felsliweg", passing by "Haus Duldeck" and walking directly towards the main entrance.

As a rule, an axis of symmetry — in accordance with the organic form principle — is common to Steiner's buildings, which all turn to face the main building. Further, we observe that utility structures such as the "Heizhaus", the "Verlagshaus" or the "Glashaus" are sited rather close together on the north side, whereas private houses lie more to the south. This arrangement in zones finds its correspondence in the functional disposition within the main building itself. The northern entrance on the shadow side is provided with larger door openings, so that scenery and other stage requisites may be carried in and out of the building, whilst the southern entrance is used chiefly by those who work at the Goetheanum and who live in its vicinity. As a visitor, we also approach from the south up the main access road to arrive at the western or the southern entrance.

The Colony

How Rudolf Steiner first came to Dornach and the present development on the hill began might be described as the impact of fate. In the autumn of 1912 he gave a lecture in Basel — not for the first time — and asked an enthusiastic friend of anthroposophical work, the dentist, Dr. Emil Grosheintz, who had already won his confidence a year earlier, whether he could suggest a quiet place of work for himself and for Marie von Sivers in the neighbourhood. The summer house of the Grosheintz family — "Haus Brodbeck" — was placed at their disposal. Thus Steiner made his first visit to Dornach on 2 October of the same year, 1912.

Grosheintz had purchased land on the hill with the intention of establishing an agricultural school there at some time in the future. His plans changed, however, when financial aid from numerous sources, chiefly from his colleague, Professor Gysi, made it possible to commence with the design and construction of an anthroposophical centre on this site, where there had previously only been a few scattered houses among the meadows.

In the spring of 1913, after it had finally become clear that the building could not be erected in Munich, a start was made in adapting the first Goetheanum and its ancillary buildings to the Dornach site. The first buildings to be erected were the "Schreinerei" (the carpenter's shop) to handle the great quantities of constructional timber and the studio for work on the coloured glass windows, the "Glashaus". Shortly afterwards the shell for the "Heizhaus" and "Haus Duldeck" for the Grosheintz family, both of reinforced concrete, were added. By 1914 the project was so far advanced that a number of people expressed the wish to build houses around the main building and be thus identified with the way of life evolving in Dornach.

In this situation Rudolf Steiner recognized the possibility of creating a model settlement, every detail of which could be carefully conceived. The plan to found a colony in Dornach was of the greatest urgency just before the outbreak of the First World War, and many interested parties had already submitted house projects. Provoked by these plans, Rudolf Steiner found it necessary to clarify the situation. He insisted that it was not a question of building "gingerbread houses" in Gothic, antique or any other historical style, but of seeking forms which would be appropriate to the present time and to the conditions peculiar to Dornach. These houses centred on the Goetheanum were to represent a completely new beginning. He wished to be able to present the world with an artistic whole.

As to the principles of planning, he uttered the following thoughts, at one and the same time eminently, almost naïvely practical and satisfying to the artistic and social sense alike. "I might say that if we know how much space is available, the purpose the space is to fulfil, how many kinds of entrance, which outlook a person requires, and if further we are precisely acquainted with the site and the relationship of a building to the Johannesbau (First Goetheanum), then we will be able to find for every situation a corresponding architecture."[26]

Such thoughts concerning the realization of a colony presumed genuine enthusiasm. This community had to set an example, not only outwardly but also in its inner relationships. Through a common spiritual intuition something was to be set in the world, pointing to possibilities for the future. Thus it was Steiner's intention to give the whole such a futuristic form that

the pioneering nature of these structures would live on in the spirit of mankind as well. The colony, as a permanent place of residence and work, was also to be legally guaranteed. In Dornach everything was related to the thought of a central building, and more precisely to one with cultural and spiritual aims. With each new structure erected according to Steiner's designs, this goal became more evident. The tendency to take up the theme of the main building and to transform it as if in a musical variation was everywhere in evidence.

To ensure that an organic building conception be accomplished, Steiner proposed the founding of a commission. The war, however, prevented the colony from being realized, as many of the interested parties came from countries involved in the struggle. During the war those in Dornach were occupied with the task of completing the first Goetheanum. Not until 27 November 1921 was it possible to issue the statutes for the "Colony at the Goetheanum in Dornach", by which the conditions of ownership within the colony were legally regulated in an appropriate manner. The architectural character of buildings to be erected on their own land subsequently had to meet with the approval of the governing board of the Anthroposophical Society.

Later records about developments on the hill are scanty. We gain the impression from a letter to the German architect and town planner, Walter Schwagenscheidt, who in 1922 had sent Rudolf Steiner drawings and textual material relating to his conception of town planning, that Steiner was not wholly satisfied with many aspects of this development in Dornach: "A little colony ought to have come about in the vicinity of the Goetheanum. The war prevented this. At the time it was still being considered, I was thinking primarily of the architecture of the immediate neighbourhood and intended to let the character of the individual buildings grow out of this terrain. But subsequently one person or another built his dwelling according to his own special idea and his supposed special needs; and that of course led to the horrors that can only disappear if thoughts such as those you entertain can be spread within the consciousness of the community at large. From this you will see that your idea lies close to my heart. Yet how can the will, or rather the will-atoms of those who want to or have to build be united under one flag?

"Your idea of the 'Dwelling-Industry-Commerce-Township' is undoubtedly justified; furthermore the garden areas; the happy idea of the cul-de-sac system, etc., but all this must first be taken up by the social will. Whoever has seen how hard it is to achieve this in a circle of people that at least harmonizes in point of a philosophy of life also sees the difficulties that stand in the way of realizing such an excellent principle as you advance in this sentence: 'The spiritual content is primary, the material form secondary.' The struggle with the client over this principle is really a tough one. And I have only had to fight it in a limited number of cases."[27]

This is a drastic mode of expression which has to be understood correctly. For Rudolf Steiner it was a disappointment to find that confidence was lacking in the practical effectiveness of the anthroposophical approach, and that some settlers stuck to conventional design. The "horrors" referred to in the letter are those private residences which were based on outmoded ideas and implied a betrayal of the whole pioneering venture. But there is, as we have seen, enough of the original intention realized in the central group on the site, to gain an impression of the significance of what had been initiated.

A Sense for Building Material: Concrete

This account would not be complete if it confined itself to fundamental aims and matters of design. All talk of a new impulse in building would be idle if the building materials themselves were not taken seriously. But we have seen that this important principle has not been ignored. The founder of the Goetheanum particularly emphasized that it is important to apply contemporary materials in the right way. And concrete, which has to undergo so many mechanically-induced processes and chemical transformations before it is *in situ* and has set, is precisely such a material. A spirited connoisseur of architectural matters, Erich Schwebsch, would wax enthusiastic about these processes when he showed that the raw materials needed to produce cement — lime and clay — must pass through the four stages of the elementary states, that used to be termed earth, water, air and fire. "Thanks to cement, man himself can make a stone!" he would exclaim. By using this new building material in place of an "old, conventional" one (which would be inappropriate or even false for producing a plastic continuity of surface), it must be so totally transformed that it again harmonizes with what is living and creating. This could not happen of itself since such a material is divorced from life and growth or indeed from the whole of nature. Hence the attempt must be made to approach the living, creative process in another way, bringing forth appropriate new shapes from the very source. This can only be done out of insight and artistic sensitivity.

Thus Rudolf Steiner was happy that this material could be used at least for the substructure of the first Goetheanum, as well as for the separate "Heizhaus" belonging to it, which housed the central heating and electrical plant.

There are people whose attention is riveted on the negative qualities of building materials. In the case of concrete, they think above all of its high absorptivity, its screening of high-frequency radiation and poor thermal insulation. They fix on a possible skin irritation occasioned (rarely) by some types of cement, and see in every building a Faraday cage which could result from the use of the steel reinforcement. Obsessed by such possibilities, these people are led to abandon the field of actual observation and to make assertions about concrete which do not stand up to scrutiny. Such pessimists should not overlook the steps which can be taken to counteract the negative qualities – there is no building material that has not got any. Apart from the obvious need for insulation, the chief measure is simply to provide *the right form*. The significance of a sensibly and artistically conceived environment for a feeling of well-being is vastly underrated, if it is taken into account at all, by those fascinated by the negative. A living, organic shaping of concrete can in this case atone in large measure for the debasement of materials derived from nature.

The artist-architect is not exonerated from striving after accuracy in these matters. He has much to learn from a statement such as the following, written from the scientific point of view.

It was kindly furnished by Dr. Florian Göbel, a faculty member of the Natural Science Section at the Goetheanum, who is at present also active in the Department of Natural Sciences at the University of Göttingen. On 9 April 1971, Göbel wrote:

"Reinforced concrete is in many respects a screening material. The steel introduced as mesh or rods in the structural members of an entire building may form a Faraday cage, that is to say, the electromagnetic fields outside it do not penetrate the interior or do so only feebly and unevenly. This applies more to buildings with a structural shell, less to those with a structural skeleton. With reference to human psychology, I recall that a certain fatigue-effect is supposedly induced when a person is largely withdrawn from the stimulating effect of electro-magnetic fields, as for example in an automobile.

"The great specific density of concrete also leads to a strong absorption of particles, especially cosmic rays.

"Related to the high specific mass is the great specific heat of concrete walls, which evens out the daily temperature curve. During our waking hours we live in the warm phase of the atmospheric sheath or in the warmth of heated spaces. Due to the large warmth capacity of concrete, the night coolness is conserved in the walls. In this respect it is important to note that in our sense of warmth we stand in a strongly reciprocal relationship to the surface temperature of the surrounding walls. The reason for this is the continuous exchange of heat by radiation, which allows us to sense the coolness of the walls, even when the air in the room is warm. Thus a certain 'screening of the climate of the living space' from the climate outside results, which is certainly quite marked as soon as moisture condenses in the concrete.

"By applying thermal insulation (Heraklith, Styropor, etc.) to one or both sides of concrete elements, we attain more favourable surface temperatures. The storage capacity has thus been neutralized, i.e. the heat exchange has been weakened by insulation.

"I consider it to be quite possible to take 'finer qualities' into consideration. If this is to be done by experiment — which has the advantage but also the disadvantage of outward objectification — then I would recommend reference being made to the researches of Joachim Schultz. In his study, *Effect of the Time of Day on Growth and Substantial Processes*,[28] Schultz describes the shielding effect produced by various materials against the qualitative effects appertaining to morning, midday, afternoon and night-time. Products of living nature, such as wood, cork, etc., were investigated; but not concrete. The observations were directed to plant growth and copper-chloride crystallization.

"The psychosomatic self-observation of man is certainly a subtler, but for that reason a more direct possibility for acquiring evidence. . . . I consider that such spaces (constructed of reinforced concrete) are more strongly isolated, fall more fully out of their surroundings. . . The Goetheanum, as a representative concrete building, affords a wonderful compensation in the unfolding forms of the west front with its great staircase.

"In these remarks I certainly do not wish to criticize reinforced concrete as a building material. The strong individualization of architecturally enclosed space which seems to be possible with this material satisfies a fundamental demand of building. Where this is intended, it should be possible by means of modelling, articulation and aperture to create a proper balance."

A year later, Göbel added to this discussion, "A clear and adequate conceptual formulation or content for peripheral forces will only emerge, therefore, when man learns to interpret the changing conditions of his own being. And to be able to understand, for example, the experiments of Schultz, a practised conceptual content is required, to avoid succumbing to all sorts of illusions."

To go further into the correspondence on this subject and the interchange of opinion between qualified persons would require a special treatise.

The fact that it is difficult in such a complicated process as building to isolate the effect of a single factor from that of other factors must not deter us from schooling our observation in the sense indicated.

Reinforced Concrete and a Utility Building

In the "Heizhaus" (central heating plant), Steiner, as an architect, was able for the first time to tackle the design of an all-concrete building. At that time, he often referred to concrete as an unresponsive material: "It is remarkably difficult to evolve concrete buildings of a suitable and genuinely artistic character, and the solution to this problem is very demanding." To develop appropriate forms for concrete and convert them into organic shapes in the round, Rudolf Steiner executed wax models to which his collaborators could refer. He favoured this procedure on good grounds.

If we are to show how a seemingly dumb and unresponsive material like concrete can be made to speak, how it can become eloquent, it seems justified to quote in detail Rudolf Steiner's relevant remarks. In Berlin, early in 1914, in connection with the colony

115

evolving in Dornach, he explained: "As a second building which has already found a definite form, we must consider the 'Heizhaus'. This structure certainly had to be conceived in the contemporary material, in reinforced concrete. The problem presented was how to execute its soaring chimney which, if it were done in the ordinary way, would certainly be an atrocity; how, too, to bring it architecturally into relationship with the main structure in a suitable building material. From the little model and the drawing you will see how an attempt has been made to find the right architectural form. When it is finally erected, especially when the furnaces are in use – for the smoke is included in the architectural concept! – then, despite its prosaic purpose, an appropriate beauty of form will perhaps be felt through the fact that the function of the building comes to real expression through it, that the form is not determined by the customary attitude to utility buildings, but that an aesthetic modelling has taken place out of the inner nature of the task. In linking the two little domes with an adjoining mass that is shaped differently in the different directions and culminates in the chimney in 'leaflike' forms (one member compared them to ears) – through all these forms it should be possible for us to experience that even a building serving the modern purpose of central heating (the Johannesbau or Goetheanum and its neighbouring premises will be heated from here), that even such a building can be given an aesthetically satisfying form. In a case like this it is necessary first of all to be fully acquainted with the purpose and content of the building."[26]

Seven years later, in a lantern lecture held in Berne, it is said of the same building: "We were really forced to design it according to the intractable nature of concrete; and true to aesthetic law and artistic feeling, we had to say to ourselves: here the starting point is the necessary heating and lighting technology. Here is the nut, around which the shell has to be built, that will draw off the smoke. This principle of 'nutshell building', if I may use this trivial expression, is carried out consistently. And whoever feels critical should consider what would otherwise have come about if the attempt had not been made – even if it is perhaps not wholly successful. There would be a towering red chimney in its place!" Then follows the significant remark: "Basically a utility building has to be created by first of all acquiring the essential feeling for the material, and then by developing the shell out of the given purpose."[29]

In evaluating such utterances, the reader must always bear in mind that Steiner was addressing lay audiences whose wakeful support he aimed to solicit without imposing upon them, and that he himself was no lover of professional jargon.

Already the model of the "Heizhaus" shows it was designed for concrete and also that its designer demanded a great deal from the material when he ventured on such bold forms. But he had to make such high demands if his concept was to be realized. Ole Falk Ebbell, as structural engineer, was equal to the task. The construction year was 1915.

This structure with its up-thrusting chimney lies to the north-east of the Goetheanum, where the steeply sloping ground had to be levelled to provide an acceptable, if still somewhat inclined site. The two buildings are joined by a path leading past lofty pine trees (and an underground duct). Hazel bushes surround the "Heizhaus" on three sides. This building can also be reached by way of the Hügelweg which continues on up to the Goetheanum.

The two little cupolas of the "Heizhaus", where neither predominates, seemed to respond to the dual motif of the great domes on the hill above it, as well as

91   The "Heizhaus" from the south-east.

92   The "Heizhaus". Wax model by Rudolf Steiner. End of 1913.

93   The "Heizhaus" freed of its scaffolding. In the rear the first Goetheanum under construction. 6. 2. 1915.

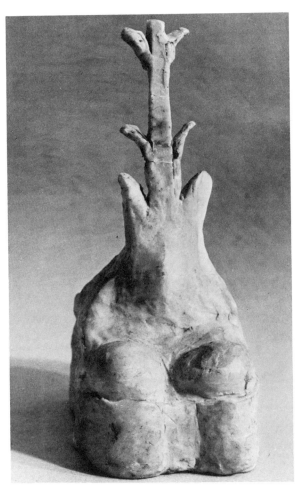

to the semi-cylindrical pylons flanking the three ground-floor entrances of the first Goetheanum. These small domes are cradled in the body of the building, behind which the chimney arises. Whilst the entrance front comprises rounded forms, the rear, rectangular on plan, and more facetted in character, has a stabilizing effect in the sloping landscape. The flanks hold these two elements — the rounded and the square — together, and, where the two poles meet, the chimney rises stage by stage, as plane surfaces give way to curved ones. Each of the three stages terminates in a pair of laterally projecting forms. The surrounds to the window openings, furnished with opaque, blue-tinted glass, repeat this motif, at the same time pointing outwards and curving downwards, with fitting understatement (Ill. 95).

The formal composition, in which the two cupolas are reduced to insignificance by the dominating, upward-shooting chimney as the *leitmotif*, is symmetrical on one axis. The lower part, composed of more prismatic forms, is plastered. The upper, more freely modelled part allows, or rather allowed, the concrete to speak — for in the course of a renovation after fifty years of use, this also had to be plastered over.

Thus this building reveals its secret to the beholder, as its creator hoped it would. An "appropriate beauty" has indeed come into being through finding a truly honest though not unimaginative shell for technical processes — combustion in the boiler, circulation in the piping, the rising and even branching of smoke, the transformation of electric current. This distinct expression was also necessary to enable an unencumbered architectural development of the main building, which was to be released from just those forces represented in the heating plant.

Here a principle is at work which deserves imitation.

96 *The "Heizhaus" from the north-east, in the rear the second Goetheanum.*

97 *The "Heizhaus". Partial view from the south.*

A Dwelling of Reinforced Concrete

A short pathway leads from the main entrance of the Goetheanum in the west along its axis to the brink of the hill. It ends in a small, rounded area where five benches were placed for the visitor's quiet contemplation of the receptive gesture of the west front with the Gempen lying behind. The Philosophers' Walk, already mentioned, leads from here down the hill, as does a second branching pathway. A vantage point affords a splendid view over Dornach and the spreading valley of the Birs, up to the ridge of the Blauen and to the Landskrone in the distance where the sun sinks in the west. If we set out from the Goetheanum along this axial pathway, we notice "Haus Duldeck", built on the rim of the hill. This house is the only other building to lie at approximately the same level as the Goetheanum. It is conspicuous for its bold and flowing forms. In its entire composition, it opens out towards a Goetheanum which no longer exists, and which would have responded to it in the appropriate language of forms.

The first impression is that of the recess in the centre of the facade, two storeys in height, surmounted by an arch. This impression is enhanced by the tower-like cylindrical features at the front corners. We sense that behind this recess a bright room with favourable lighting conditions must extend through the depth of the house. If we walk around the house, we see more clearly that this is actually the case, for a similar arched recess opens on the valley side, here flanked immediately by small tower-like projections. The consequence of this recessing is that the central, ground-floor room is relatively small in size, but appears much larger due to its windows and the prospect gained. The true theme of the building seems to be just this: to open itself to and form a "passage" for what emanates from the main building.

The two lower storeys are separated by the modelled profile of a belt encircling the building at the height of the ground-floor ceiling. We observe in this girdle an attempt to bring to expression the various directions of movement implied by the plan. This is achieved by modelling it with unequal emphasis. It permits the lower part of the building to share the plastic life of the whole. On the eastern face it presses close against the wall, follows the curve of the semi-cylindrical structures and at the transition from cylindrical to flat wall raises itself in the corner, as if to serve a double function: to protect the lower parts of the wall from the elements and to underline the dynamic of movement tending inwards and upwards. To the west, this girdle makes an opposite movement at the half-turrets, tending downwards. The undersides of the balconies built into the arched niches take up the form of the belt, so that it serves as an element binding the whole building together. Even the lintel over the door in the asymmetrical main entrance to the north-west connects itself with the girdling moulding, seeming to lend the entrance its full motivation (Ill. 107).

In connection with the rebuilding of the Goetheanum, reference has been made to "Haus Duldeck" and its "concrete style". The strongly modelled roof of this house was also executed in reinforced concrete and indicates most clearly the principles of form which guided Rudolf Steiner. To the north-east more concave forms prevail, as if the roof had been "impressed" by the portal motif of the main building opposite; to the south-west, overlooking the valley, the roof is corbelled out in a massive swelling and convex forms predominate. This polarity is to be noted in every aspect of the house, from the disposition of the parts on plan to the detailing of cornices and mouldings, balconies, doors, openings in the roof, the chimney, and the charming forms of the outside steps. It is the design of steps and stairways in particular which reveals the inexhaustible architectural fantasy of Rudolf Steiner, his "play urge" in Schiller's sense, free yet restrained.

The two doorways deserve special study, for they were executed faithfully according to the models. The asymmetrical doorway to the north-west has already been mentioned; the other, to the south-east, is symmetrical and incorporated more into the surface of the southern wall.

The concrete outer walls have been plastered and are furnished with an inner layer of hollow tile by way of thermal insulation. The trussed roof-construction is partly clad with concrete, and partly — as is so often the case with Steiner's buildings — covered with slate.

The interior of "Haus Duldeck" is determined by the symmetrical layout of the two lower storeys. Here the rooms follow one another in organic sequence so that no connecting passage is required, despite the fact that the stairway is located in the north-western part of the house. At roof level, however, where — as an after-thought — the rooms were conceived rather for board-ing guests, a central corridor has been introduced. These rooms are for the most part sunny and, in their colour treatment, Rudolf Steiner took the opportunity to apply transparent coatings of paint to the walls. In the thirties one of the authors saw the original red coating in the main room at first-floor level before it had to be painted over. This colour treatment had been personally supervised by Steiner and in part executed by him. Carl Kemper gave an eye-witness account: "A pail of the thin, almost transparent red paint or 'glaze' was standing on the floor beside a ladder. Dr. Steiner took a broad brush, dipped it into the paint, shook it out on the edge of the paint-pot until the brush was fairly dry and weighed it for a moment in his hand; he then climbed the ladder and held the brush on the wall under the ceiling. Slowly and surely he drew the brush straight down the wall until he reached the floor. Then he repeated the whole procedure. He seemed to ponder exactly how much suction the plaster would exert — for it was not easy to reach an even result. We did not have the right materials and a striped effect was hardly to be avoided. But Dr. Steiner succeeded remarkably well. It was as if he had already had a good deal of practice."[30]

This example illustrates that our experience of a building will only be complete if the sense of life contributed by the right forms be supplemented by transparent colours imbuing the interior with a real soul element.

To the first planning period of the house in 1913—14 belongs a wax model from Rudolf Steiner's hand, that has since partially collapsed. Despite the damage, it may be seen that originally a built-out roof storey did not belong to the programme and that at the design stage the area and volume of the body of the house probably predominated over its height and the pitched roof more than they do in the executed job. Before construction began, the owner requested a number of alterations. Steiner obliged and modified his design accordingly. The tower-like corner rooms thus evolved from simple rounded protrusions. Balconies were integrated into the design of the arched recesses, the north-eastern balcony particularly being formed in such

104 "Haus Duldeck". Side entrance facing south-east.

105 "Haus Duldeck". Detail of outdoor steps facing south-west.

106   *"Haus Duldeck". Rudolf Steiner's wax model for the
main entrance to the north-west. 1914.*

107   *"Haus Duldeck". Main entrance to the north-west, as executed.*

a way that it did not have a disturbing effect on the vault above. And finally, so that the possibility might exist of renting rooms in the house, Steiner permitted the attic storey to be adapted to further living accommodation. The house thus acquired fifteen rooms on completion but, as opposed to the original conception, a modified appearance.

Today the house serves the purposes of a publisher and book shop, although until recently it remained in the possession of the family for whom it was built.

Stages of Construction on the Hill

"Haus Duldeck", the "Glashaus" and the "Heizhaus", together with the double-domed first Goetheanum, not only represented a recognizable architectural whole, but also terminated the construction period extending from 1913 to 1916. No further building projects were commenced during the war and it was only with great difficulty that "Haus Duldeck" could be brought to completion. All available forces were expended rather on the completion of the interior of the main building.

The next construction period could not begin until 1919–20 and went on until 1923. It was concerned chiefly with the building of private houses which were consequently not handled by the construction office at the Goetheanum. Paul Bay and others offered their services to help bring Rudolf Steiner's domestic designs to realization. Bay had had a sculptor's training in Munich and did not turn his attention to architecture until he arrived in Dornach.

Strictly speaking, this was not a period devoted to building in concrete. Indeed it is only worth mentioning in a study of the architecture of reinforced concrete in that by other, certainly less expensive means — brick with a timber backing and plastic skin — a technique was applied which to a certain extent bore a modelled character suited to concrete and attempted to speak its language. But since all these buildings adjacent to the Goetheanum, although originating with Rudolf Steiner, were handled in detail by others,[31] they are introduced here only for the sake of completeness.

The three "Eurythmiehäuser" south-east of the main building were the first to be erected. These three similar but not identical residences were designed with the help of models jointly by Rudolf Steiner and his assistant, the English sculptress Edith Maryon, who, with her particular bent, enjoyed being involved in an architectural project. The models were then interpreted in Bay's office. Although they are not of concrete, they have significance in the general development of the site around the Goetheanum. Their compactness and modest scale serve to emphasize the significance of the main building in the landscape. Because of their location they are not so obviously oriented to the Goetheanum as are the other ancillary buildings, but are related more to the view.

In addition the private dwellings "Haus Vreede" 1919 and "Haus van Blommestein" 1920 must be mentioned, even though they stand in no direct relation to the Goetheanum Hill.

The most important project in Bay's office was the execution of the impressive "Haus de Jaager" 1921, opposite the southern wing of the Goetheanum, but standing on a lower-lying part of the site. At first glance we recognize that the building must serve two functions. The block rising from a square-shaped ground plan encloses a studio and effectively takes up one of the often repeated themes of Steiner's buildings — a recessed facade with flanking corner pilasters. The studio lying to the north is embraced by the living quarters to the south, two storeys high. These two distinct masses express a two-fold concept: the relationship between living and working. From the professional point of view it is a pity the house was not constructed completely in concrete, for its character would lend itself admirably to this material. But even built in rendered brick it makes a telling impression as an eloquent, articulated whole. The colour of the external plaster corresponds to the massing of the building, the higher studio block being reddish, the living quarters bluish. This side of the work was supervised by Felix Durach, then active in Bay's office. Rudolf Steiner's original design was modified during the planning period upon the owner's request to afford a mezzanine area lit by the noonday sun.

Not only its exterior but also its interior is well worth closer inspection. Here the qualities of light from subdued to radiantly bright are present. A "eurythmic" sense for space breathes through the whole interior, drawing together and spreading out, contracting and expanding, breaking away and reuniting, opening itself and closing again, according to its function. In the studio valuable works by the Belgian sculptor, Jacques de Jaager, are on permanent exhibition. There remains a free floor space for the practice of eurythmy, visible speech and visible song, here proving to be sculpture translated into living movement. Something unfolds

like a breath of Ancient Greece, reborn in a modern guise.

The diffuse light falls from the strikingly shaped north window in the vaulted ceiling and fills the violet-tinted space, stimulating concentrated artistic work. Does this mood and treatment not indicate that not only sculpture but also architecture stands to gain from this new art of movement? That the sculptural element, animated by a language made visible by eurythmy, might also with advantage find admittance into architecture? That building forms might also give voice,

and that this aim might be fulfilled with concrete as the appropriate building material? Without man's gift for creating forms, without his technical ability, concrete remains formless. Through the exercise of these capacities, it might speak an eloquent language, unencumbered by words. Can it be right to force concrete, with its mouldable attributes, into the strait-jacket of outmoded, geometrically determined norms? Does not contemporary practice deny man something to which he is in fact entitled in this century?

Whilst we have lingered a moment in the artistic atmosphere of this studio, questions have been formulated in our consciousness such as this young sculptor might have raised before his untimely death in 1915. Rudolf Steiner gave an encouraging and generally applicable answer when he wrote these words beneath an "eurythmically" executed charcoal sketch by Jacques de Jaager:

Des Geistes Schattenwurf im Raume
ist das Schöne.
Der Schatten wird zum Lebewesen durch des
Künstlers Bildegeist.

Beauty is the shadow cast by the spirit in space;
The shadow becomes a living being through the
artist's formative spirit.

The "Transformatorenhaus" on the Herzental-strasse belongs to the same construction period as "Haus de Jaager" and was carried out by the same office. Steiner's sketches and indications aimed to make visible the conversion of electricity, in this case alternating current. The planning carried out in 1921 fell to a young associate, Helmuth Lauer, who later established a distinguished practice based on Stuttgart.

The building of the second Goetheanum belongs to

the third construction period, commencing in 1923 after a short pause. It represents a climax in concrete construction on the Dornach hill. In the meantime Paul Bay had moved away from Dornach. Shortly after this the first Goetheanum was destroyed by fire, causing a completely new situation to arise. No longer could a twin-domed building be considered for the central theme. We must assume that after the fire Rudolf Steiner gave much thought to the concept of the new Goetheanum and its erection, and it soon became apparent that he wished it to accommodate a greater variety of activities than had been possible in the first building. To a certain degree it would thus become more of an "all-purpose" building.

First to be built in the year 1923 was the "Eurythmeum", already intimating the forms of the new Goetheanum. This building nestles in the landscape in such a way that only its roof-surfaces are visible from the Goetheanum. If we approach the "Eurythmeum" from the north-west, however, and raise our eyes, we see how its pair of pillars to the west take up the supporting theme of the main building. As Rudolf Steiner himself writes, the conception of the new Goetheanum occupied his mind for a year.[32] It may therefore be assumed that whilst the Eurythmeum was being planned and executed, he was already contemplating the future main building. Hence the design differed in character from the earlier structures, not only because of a new purpose but also because of a new dialogue which was to be established between the new buildings without destroying the harmony of the whole.

Approaching the "Eurythmeum", which forms the northern section of the present Rudolf Steiner Halde, from the Goetheanum, we move west past "Haus Duldeck", veer north and find ourselves on a narrow approach which leads directly to the "Halde". What we first see behind the thick-set trees is not a typical "Rudolf Steiner house" but one which was vaguely reminiscent of the Renaissance tradition before it was replastered. The house was formerly called "Brodbeck" and is the oldest on the hill, as the original drawings for this — to put it mildly — architecturally insignificant chalet date back to 1905. It was here that Rudolf Steiner stayed in 1912 as a guest of the Grosheintz family. In 1921 the house, which did not suit its surroundings, was taken over for anthroposophical purposes. The first thought was certainly to do away with it altogether. Instead, it experienced gradual alteration, and the extension under discussion, which represented a new stage in Steiner's architectural creativity. To build the extension and maintain the same floor level, the land north of the existing villa had to be raised and terraced. Thus a monumental escarpment was set upon the original sloping meadow, an undoubted advantage for the total impression in the landscape. Here the "Eurythmeum" was placed, built according to its purpose in the form of a rectangle of classic proportions. At ground level it consisted of a single large practice room for eurythmy, recitation and drama; in the upper storey, a studio was furnished for the donor of the building, the Dutch artist Meta Waller. A simple connecting block mediates between the old and the new structure.

A study of this building soon leads to the observation that, in contrast to the others constructed by Rudolf Steiner, it is asymmetrical. This fact is an honest consequence of its being added on to the existing house. The principle of compensation and balance had to be taken into account. In addition, the basement level is emphasized more strongly in this building than in earlier structures as a plinth, underlining the aim of

maintaining balance and seeming to anchor the building more firmly to the ground, as is appropriate on a sloping site.

In this design it is difficult to say whether its particular asymmetrical quality results from a swinging out of symmetry or from a struggle to re-establish symmetry.

Viewed from the west, two characteristic piers supporting the roof are placed in front of the practice room, and above them, at the same time bearing downwards and jutting upwards, is an equally expressive roof formation with a pair of windows modelled into it. A transition between this new part and the old is formed by a covered terrace and entrance, the sinuous line of the cornice to the overhanging roof evolving from a corbel which appears to cling to the angle of the existing wall. The wide steps and projecting base, which seem to welcome the visitor, both prove rewarding objects of study (Ills. 3, 119, 122).

The longer side faces north with a beautifully modelled entrance approximately halfway, integrated with the window opening above. This entrance leads directly into the practice room. To its left and right windows of unequal size have been set, and on the far right at the corner one of the previously mentioned projecting columns is situated, which supports the extension of the upper storey into the roof space.

To the east, overlooking the Goetheanum, the wall openings in both storeys are larger in relationship to the wall surface than those of the other faces of the building. They thus acquire a different character and significance, being more abrupt and severe (Ill. 116).

Everywhere we encounter the principle of compensation, balancing out rather than symmetry. The lively and at the same time controlled modelling of the northern entrance, together with the front steps and the subtle slant of the various roof surfaces, makes it a sculptural masterpiece.

Regarding the standard of execution of the ancillary buildings, Rudolf Steiner could only give his wholehearted approval to the "Eurythmeum". The sculptor Oswald Dubach and the architect Ernst Aisenpreis had mounted the scaffolding and, with the help of hazel rods, had interpreted the sculptural forms of the model full size for the benefit of the bricklayers, concreters and plasterers. Steiner called this building "the infant of the Goetheanum". He was never to set eyes on the full embodiment of the "mother".

117 The "Eurythmeum". Detail of north-east entrance.

118 The "Eurythmeum" from the east.

Illustrations on pages 152 and 153

119, 120, 121 The "Eurythmeum". Rudolf Steiner's plasticine model.

122 The "Eurythmeum" from the south-west. To the right, the old "Haus Brodbeck".

As the plan to re-erect the main building matured, leading to the maquette and the resumption of the works, two further buildings were added to the general site development: the "Verlagshaus" and "Haus Schuurman".

The office and storehouse for the Philosophisch-Anthroposophischer Verlag, which was designed in the autumn of 1923, swiftly rose from the ground and was completed by January 1924. As in the case of the "Transformatorenhaus" Rudolf Steiner had only made sketches that indicated an irregular octagonal ground plan. The external walls of the somewhat raised ground floor were to enclose a single space. The architects Aisenpreis and Ranzenberger were able to report how exact Steiner was in the siting of this building — as in the relationship of all the buildings to one another — for they were present when he stood in the meadow and, looking around at nearby structures, changed the orientation which had already been staked out.

The "Verlagshaus" found its place on the Hügelweg, between the two buildings conceived a decade earlier, the "Heizhaus" and the "Glashaus". Its slate roof consists of a number of facets and rises over the octagonal — at street level actually U-shaped — floor plan. The indentation on the street side, which penetrates deeply into the building and forms an entrance niche, with a gently vaulted ceiling, creates a most powerful effect. Arranged around this recess are three larger window openings. Their unusual design lends the southern aspect (street front) a contemporary character. The other external walls are windowless and the interior is otherwise only lit by a roof-light. A cellar provides additional storage space. Above the concrete basement, the timber frame has breeze-block infilling and is rendered with a blue-grey plaster. As had been the case with the "Eurythmeum", the construction of this publishing house was supervised by the planning office at the Goetheanum, under the direction of Ernst Aisenpreis.

At some distance to the east of the main building lies the house of the Dutch musician and composer Schuurman. If living accommodation had no longer been available for him in Dornach, he, and his wife, an eurythmist, would have been forced to move away from the area. Rudolf Steiner induced them to stay, offering them a site where building had not yet taken place and where the main building was thus left relatively "unprotected" in the east. Those acquainted with Rudolf Steiner's life story, particularly in the year 1924, will be in a position to appreciate what it means that the sketches for this simple residence — the last of his essays in architecture — were completed on 29 September, on Michaelmas Day of that year. Adopting a square of eight metres, he developed a plan and elevations of strict proportions. The motif for its forms is a kind of response to the eastern aspect of the Goetheanum. It is as if the characteristic outline of the stage block had impressed itself upon the western face of the house, to provide a recessed entrance and a place for sitting outdoors in the evenings. Here indeed is a "neighbourly" relationship between one building and another.

For all its simplicity and economy, there is something satisfying about this design. Enhancing the entrance motif, the effect of the strongly projecting, crisply modelled roof surfaces is added, and their interrelationship arouses in the attentive observer the impression of a gentle beating of wings.

Before construction the depth of the building was increased by two metres, and thus the originally intended harmony of proportion has been affected. As was the case with the "Verlagshaus" the previous year, "Haus Schuurman" also has a timber frame. The outer walls are plastered; the roof planes, with folds like a

table-cloth, were covered with the glistening Norwegian slate which Steiner had seen in 1913 in the slate quarries of Voss, between Oslo and Bergen, and which hè had understandably come to love. It was used for most of the buildings to his design.

"Haus Schuurman" was completed towards the end of March 1925 and the circle of buildings, grouped immediately around the Goetheanum, was thus closed. Despite setbacks, the hill was able to demonstrate a consistently executed whole which in all its parts may be traced back to Rudolf Steiner as initiator.

Even if the project has remained germinal, even if the hopes and possibilities stimulated by the Colony have in many directions not been developed, a significant result was nevertheless achieved, and this can set an example. This is expressed not merely in the siting and design of the group of buildings, but in the way the ancillary structures are related to the main building, harmonizing with it as with their surroundings. The composition as a whole points clearly to the activities carried out under the roof of the Goetheanum, lending them their own individuality.

FUTURE PROSPECT

Frank Lloyd Wright was standing in his studio at Taliesin North, contemplating a book in his hand. *"Goethe's Conception of the World*, by Rudolf Steiner," he read. One of his young assistants, Robert Warn, who had just handed it to him, saw that he was moved. "You know, Bob, nobody has any idea how much Goethe has meant to me in my life. For me he is a true world-liberator." Then the eighty-year-old architect added, "I know about Rudolf Steiner, but I should know more." For another twelve years until his death at Easter, 1959, Wright continued to be active. Over and over again the existence of the man who had built the Goetheanum was to be recalled to his mind. Perhaps he found time for that deeper acquaintance his remark suggested. Yet the world was not to learn the outcome. It was as though with him an epoch had come to an end.

The era following on its heels awaits in its turn a "world-liberator". But it stares into a void. It is in danger of losing touch with reality and consequently of being subjected to a "world-enslaver". The arguments for disbanding the architect's profession were presented by Wolf Meyer-Christian, recently returned from Britain, in a discussion of *The Professional Plight of the Architect* (reported in *Deutsche Bauzeitung*, No. 6, 1969). "The pressure towards the development of a public economy signifies, as far as the economics of construction are concerned, and despite all arguments to the contrary, a compulsion towards total industrialization." Anyone who presumes to hold this constraint to be anything other than the very principle underlying man's future form of existence, cradles himself in utopian dreams. "The utopians are already in retreat, due to the fact that we are now able to regard predictable events as realities as soon as the requisite methods, means and times have been described." What was formerly abstract assumes the character of reality; what was reality is treated as an abstraction.

"Only by failing to take into account what he really contributes can an architect today still be blind to the fact that there are no more substances nor objects and hence no materials nor things to be constructed. In principle, nothing remains that can be identified qualitatively. On the contrary, in the process of executing something, arbitrary aggregates of information are described, and then brought together into materials according to the desired performance characteristics. The rules for this coordination are devoid of perceptible attributes; their complexity increases without their being in principle open to discussion. In the last analysis, abstracting a technical combination into a technological allocation is no longer a mental but a mechanical process. Aesthetic decisions have no further bearing in construction."

Further indications of technical progress are recognized in the fact that information concerning the rules for processing "can in practically no sphere still be expressed or transmitted in our own language. This is preferably replaced by a mathematical language appropriate to the specific problem." And: "Similarly have the concepts 'space' and 'meaning' lost their content in building. Even undynamic quantities such as the manner and cost of procurement or the type and cost of production are transformed into unique or repetitive processes analysed and rationalized by means of operational research." The introduction into this "no-man's-land" is crowned by the assertion that "design was that bygone articulation of general agreement and hence was always attached to meaning. The activity associated with it was the detailing into actual forms, whose arrangement and merging into sublimated wholes generated significance. Planning is not merely the opposite of designing; it is the methodical fulfilment of abstracted requirements through quantitative coordination.

Planning forgoes creative involvement identified with the self in favour of a decision-taking activity detached from value-judgement. It enforces thereby, in any society above a certain level of civilization, a completely new and highly complex relationship to the environment."

The essence of the questions raised here so relentlessly yet not unjustly, appears to us to lie in the sentence: "Planning forgoes creative involvement identified with the self in favour of a decision-taking activity detached from value-judgement." Whatever course is to be steered into the future, no objection can be raised against our continuing to plan and make decisions. But if this activity is supposed to be detached from any value-judgement, haven't we already lost sight of the human being who was to be served by our planning? On the other hand it should be clear that any honest contemporary would choose an activity divorced from value-judgements rather than "creative involvement" purely to satisfy his own egoism. Could there, however, really be any talk of a true creative dedication to some end if this did not originate purely in self-forgetfulness? Precisely the fact that Meyer-Christian speaks of a "forgoing" of this involvement, betrays that we should by no means detach ourselves from value-judgements. To speak of forgoing something only makes sense if there is something worthwhile for us to renounce. Would it be necessary to practise this renunciation if it were understood that the common good of mankind cannot be served without a creative involvement, a kind of devotion that only the artist knows? It is self-centredness which has to be renounced, not creativity.

The attitude arising from a one-sided application of cybernetics would put compulsion in place of conviction. But aren't such thoughts themselves compulsive? For in reality (by your leave!) there still is substance, there still is construction; materials still exist. Moreover, there really is "space" where buildings have to spread themselves. And there still exist people to whom the buildings arising in space will have to speak for a long time. But in what language?

As one alternative, we are offered a "mathematical language" which is no longer "our own language". The other alternative is a language of forms communicating immediately with the spirit of man from a building that embraces him as does the Goetheanum, the "House of Speech", whose forms call for further partners in conversation. There are men who develop a sense for this language, who recognize it as untranslatable and indispensable, and who would like to learn to understand it still more intimately. They will have nothing more to do with abstractions. They seek concrete advice as to how, in some responsible way, they can be creatively active in the service of their fellow men through building. For such people, who are seeking a "true world-liberator", the following remarks aim to sketch a future prospect illustrating a further aspect of the Goetheanum's mission. Hints are given for the practice and understanding of art, which can be applied by any individual or group; ways of unfolding capacities which have to be developed if a new form of architecture is to arise.

We are far from wanting to predict the course of future events in the manner indulged in by cybernetics, let alone to consider them as *faits accomplis*. Not by any form of compulsion, but only in complete freedom can these paths leading to a new architectural insight be pursued. The fruits of an architecture speaking to man of a universal harmony can only ripen if they are actively willed and created.

In the first chapter we referred to the particular interest in a spiritually inspired architecture which the Goetheanum in Dornach has stimulated amongst the younger generation. This interest inevitably leads to the question of training and practice to be made accessible to such young people if they are to develop the capacities and skills needed to build in a social way. At the same time it is a question of expanding the consciousness; a question of self-education. What the Goetheanum has to offer in meeting this situation is therefore less a contribution to discussion than a challenge to participate creatively in the self-training of those capacities which are the only assurance that there will be an architecture of the future at all.

Much that had its beginnings at the Goetheanum has remained germinal, but the seeds have been sown and need only be cultivated in order to thrive. Asked by an architect, who had observed the founding of various Sections at the School of Spiritual Science, whether there might not be a suitable training course for architects as well, Rudolf Steiner is said to have replied that he would consider it. It is clear, however, that the situation was not at that time ripe for attempting anything specific in this direction. Despite the fact that the "Bau" of the Goetheanum was also a "house" of speech, no "Bauhaus" evolved in Dornach immediately after the First World War, although this would have been quite conceivable, considering the colony that had come into being there. Thus it was for the time being left to others to realize this task – certainly with a totally different orientation. Particularly during the Weimar period of the "Bauhaus" under Gropius, the leading instructors – Kandinsky, Klee, Schreyer, Schlemmer, and others – came to discuss the anthroposophical background of the Goetheanum. But that was a long time ago.

It is pertinent to ask whether there is any incentive for cultivating architecture as an art at the Goetheanum today. The question does not leave us empty-handed. We experience that the Goetheanum is not merely a building but that it harbours an active, self-renewing impulse that can lead on into the future. Characteristic of its approach is not merely to record results – such as the building itself – but also to indicate the pathway leading to them. This is the ingredient of educational method that is always essential to continuity. Such stimulation for the cultivation and renewal of architecture issues from the Goetheanum continuously, and it has already proved fruitful. Below we list some of the factors contributing to this cultivation of architecture as the Goetheanum understands it, whether through the beginnings of a recognizable training, through occasional courses, weekend conferences, workshops or through independent work and study:

1. The Goetheanum itself, including its ancillary buildings.
2. The models, drawings and ideas that have led to these buildings.
3. Becoming aware of the forces active in architecture (load and support, etc.), using all available means.
4. Cultivating a feeling for plastic spatial forms by modelling.
   Negative and positive (concave and convex) forms.
   Doubly-curved surfaces (semblance of the living).
   Metamorphosis (semblance of the conscious).
   School of Sculpture.
5. Study and demonstration of the fundamental phenomena of so-called projective geometry.
   Space and counter-space – Correspondence – Transformation – Involution.
   Section for Mathematics and Astronomy.
   Institute for Mathematics and Physics.
6. Anthropological studies of architecture and building construction with regard to man and his environment (ecological approach).

Transformation of the old concept of functionalism by inclusion of the human being in the formulation of the task.

"You ask yourself, what happens?" (Rudolf Steiner). The finding of the motif.

7. Eurythmy (visible speech, visible song). "Soul gymnastics." Qualitative spatial experience. Dynamics of movement.

8. Theory of colour (Goethe, Steiner). "Colour perspective." The relation of colour and image to architectural space.
Transparent paint and its application.
Plant colours and their production.
Training in artists' ateliers.
Fine Arts Section.

9. The principle of metamorphosis. Application in planning and design.

10. Extended study of Goetheanistic natural science.
"The power of judgement during the act of observation" (Goethe).
Earth and cosmos: man's relationship to them.
Development of a feeling for materials by overcoming materialism.
Natural Science Section.

11. Art theory. "Reconciliation of the arts".
Origin and task of architecture.
Evolution of architecture as a reflection of inner spiritual history.
Section for Aesthetic Science.

12. The threefold division of the social organism.
Architecture within the free spiritual life and in the economic life.
The life of rights: keeping the balance.
Relationship of architect to owner.
Group work and social practice.
New economic concepts and skills.
Healthy agriculture and landscaping.

Section for Social Science; Section for Agriculture and Food Research.

13. Architecture and technology.
Further development of reinforced concrete. Fair-faced concrete.
Formwork.
The etching of coloured glass.

14. Basic study of man and education.
Their implication in school construction.
Pedagogical Section.

To simplify access to these areas, a bibliography is appended.

Apart from the other Sections of the School of Spiritual Science referred to, the Fine Arts Section co-ordinates all activities relevant to architecture. It should, however, be realized that the School of Spiritual Science is not confined to Dornach and that many aspects of this work are cultivated elsewhere.

The indications given are not intended as a programme. It should be clear that the areas mentioned are not sufficient in themselves for a curriculum in architecture but rather supplement or expand in directions which have become essential and are being demanded by the needs of young people.

And if we have broached the subject of training, it is not with the intention of maintaining or furthering those institutions whose usefulness has already become questionable. Rather must capacities be developed through original work to apply moral fantasy and moral technique in the field of architecture. What is necessary is practice – individually and in groups.

In so far as this applies to training in art schools, we are able to shed light on the matter through conversations drawn from real life.

A. Are you finishing at the art academy this summer?
B. I hope so. I'd like to. The problem is that we have to

hand in our final project as a group, so it doesn't just depend on me.

A. What kind of a project is it?

B. We have the choice: a concert hall or a community centre.

A. You're surely not expected to do more than the interior design? You will be able to choose from various designs for the buildings themselves?

B. No, that's just it. We have to do the plans and all the drawings first, and that's really difficult, since we've learnt nothing about architecture as such.

A. Aren't you given any basis?

B. No, none at all.

(A. believes that there is still something to be learned from the art of the past.)

A. Hm. When does world history begin for you?

B. (Smiling enigmatically) With Mies van der Rohe.

A. I might have known. But surely you have been taken through recent history — William Morris, the pioneers of industrial architecture and town planning, the Impressionists, Art Nouveau, the Expressionists, the "Bauhaus" era and so forth?

B. We've never had that. We don't have lectures.

A. (taking a deep breath) But you have at least been given an extensive reading programme?

B. No, really not. Our professors have never recommended anything.

(A. thought of the many tasks in mural painting, for which the younger generation would have to be prepared . . . presumably in art schools.)

*

N. reports: At a meeting of colour consultants for the town X, they saw that my attitude to the problems was not the customary one, and that I was battling for a living approach. A professor at the academy asked me afterwards if I would hold a course for students on Goethe's theory of colour. They needed stimulation, he said; the attendance was only sporadic. I suggested not just theorizing. Perhaps I could finally do some painting with the art students? "Painting!" exclaimed the professor. "You want to paint with the art students? We gave that up a long time ago. They didn't come. But you could try it. And good luck to you! If you really pull that off . . . !"

So I began. A few came. I noticed how unobservant they were. They had not been trained to look. Essentially they were quite uneducated and at first had no questions. They gradually came to life through the phenomena themselves, and their interest grew. More came. Some students from other faculties joined as well — engineers, for example. In the end we painted together, and a number said they would like to continue . . .

*

In the introductory chapter we looked at the Goetheanum through the eyes of a selected number of contemporaries from the professional world of architecture. In comparing these examples, we notice the contrast between the more subjective attitude of western writers as opposed to the discipline in handling spiritual issues which is still characteristic of orientals. Yoshiro Ikehara does not begin by imposing his view on what he saw in Dornach. He considers it to be his duty first of all to take account of what has been written by those conversant with the subject and only then to pass on the undistorted results to his readers — for example, of the Japanese magazine, *Space Design* (No. 3, 1964). With admirable clarity he explains how Steiner's artistic activity arose primarily as an inner necessity of the anthroposophical movement. Only in conclusion does he write of the significance which he himself attaches to what he has described. We, too, close with these words, translated from the Japanese:

"If I think over the history of the Goetheanum; if I reflect on the seed of what is growing from research into the other side of existence, paralleling technical developments; if that time, heralded to us by so many symptoms of the present day, is really approaching us through that kind of progress in the world symbolized by modern technology — then afterwards the existence of Steiner, who appears to have lived rather apart from prevailing developments, will come towards us from the distant future of our evolution. This will, I'm sure, imprint itself deeply on my soul."

129 The Goetheanum. Terrace in the west during an interval.

ANNOTATIONS

[1] (p. 20) Shinko-Geijutsu, *On the New Goetheanum*, 2 March 1930, Tokyo.

[2] (p. 22) Rudolf Steiner, *And the Temple Becomes Man*, Rudolf Steiner Press, London, 1979.

[3] (p. 32) Rudolf Steiner, *The Architectural Conception of the Goetheanum*, Rudolf Steiner Publishing Co., London, and Anthroposophic Press, New York, 1938 (to be used with illustrations from *Der Baugedanke des Goetheanum*, Dornach, 1932).

[4] (pp. 33, 38) Heinz Müller, "Reminiscences" in *Spuren auf dem Weg*, Stuttgart, 1970, and in *Mitteilungen aus der anthroposophischen Arbeit in Deutschland*, Stuttgart, No. 26, Christmas 1953.

[5] (p. 33) See Annotation 3.

[6] (pp. 41, 42) Rudolf Steiner, *Aufbaugedanken und Gesinnungsbildung* (lecture of 21 July 1923), Dornach, 1942.

[7] (pp. 43, 44) Rudolf Steiner, "Der künftige Baugedanke von Dornach", lecture of 31 December 1923 published in *Die Weihnachtstagung zur Begründing der Allgemeinen Anthroposophischen Gesellschaft 1923–1924*, Dornach, 1963.

[8] (p. 46) Albert von Baravalle, "Das Baumotiv des zweiten Goetheanum" in *Das Goetheanum*, 31st Year, No. 12, 23 March 1952.

[9] (p. 47) Rudolf Steiner, "Zum Wiederaufbau des Goetheanums", lecture of 1 January 1924. See Annotation 7.

[10] (p. 47) *Das Goetheanum*, Special Edition of 18 December 1924.

[11] (p. 47) Ita Wegman in *Was in der Anthroposphischen Gesellschaft vorgeht*, 2nd Year, 3 May 1925, page 69.

[12] (p. 47) Indication by Dipl. Ing. Helmuth Lauer.

[13] (p. 47) See Dr. Ernst Lehrs in *Mitteilungen aus der anthroposophischen Arbeit in Deutschland*, No. 7, 1964.

[14] (p. 62) *Schweizerische Bauzeitung*, Volume 85, No. 7.

[15] (p. 65) See Carl Kemper, *Der Bau*, Stuttgart, 1966, pages 17–23.

[16] (p. 71) See *Protokoll zur 5. ordentlichen Generalversammlung des Johannesbauvereins in Dornach*, 21 October 1917, page 5.

[17] (p. 74) See *Was in der Anthroposphischen Gesellschaft vorgeht*, 4th Year, No. 26, 26 June 1927.

[18] (p. 75) Albert Steffen in *Was in der Anthroposophischen Gesellschaft vorgeht*, 5th Year, No. 47, 18 November 1928.

[19] (p. 86) Assya Turgenieff, *The Goetheanum Windows*, Rudolf Steiner Press, London, and Anthroposophic Press, New York, 1938.

[20] (p. 86) Rudolf Steiner, "Dimension, Number, Weight", lecture of 29 July 1923 in *Colour* (1935), Rudolf Steiner Publishing Co., London, and Anthroposophic Press, New York, 1935.

[21] (p. 89) Rudolf Steiner, "Die okkulten Gesichtspunkte des Stuttgarter Baues", lecture of 15 October 1911 published in *Bilder okkulter Siegel und Säulen*, Dornach, 1977.

[22] (p. 104) Rudolf Steiner, "The New Conception of Architecture", 3rd lecture in *Ways to a New Style in Architecture*, Anthroposophical Publishing Co., London, and Anthroposophic Press, New York, 1927.

[23] (p. 105) Percy MacKaye and Albert Steffen in *Das Goetheanum*, 36th Year, No. 35, 1 September 1957.

[24] (p. 109) J. W. von Goethe, *Letters from Switzerland*, 3 October 1779.

[25] (p. 110) From a manuscript by Georg Hartmann.

[26] (pp. 112, 117) Rudolf Steiner, lecture of 23 January 1914, Berlin.

[27] (p. 113) From a letter from Rudolf Steiner to Walter Schwagenscheidt of 22 July 1922, in *Blätter für Anthroposophie*, Basel.

[28] (p. 115) Joachim Schultz, *Wirksamkeit der Tageszeiten in Wachstum und Substanzgeschehen*, Dornach, 1951.

[29] (p. 117) See Annotation 3 (page 34).

[30] (p. 128) Oral communication by Carl Kemper to Rex Raab.

[31] (p. 139) Erich Zimmer, *Rudolf Steiner als Architekt von Wohn- und Zweckbauten*, Stuttgart, 1971.

[32] (p. 147) Letter from Rudolf Steiner to Dr. Gerhard Börlin (President of the Swiss National Trust), 30 December 1924.

DORNACH BUILDING CHRONICLE 1913–1971

FIRST CONSTRUCTION PERIOD

1913	July	Interior model of the first Goetheanum
1913	20 September	Laying of the foundation stone
1914	1 April	Topping-out ceremony
1914	14 July	Inauguration of the "Glashaus" (glass engraving studios)
1915		Completion of the "Heizhaus" (central heating building)
1915–16		"Haus Duldeck" (house for donors of part of Goetheanum grounds)
1914–18		Work slows down on the Goetheanum during the First World War
1920	September	Opening of the first Goetheanum (still incomplete)

SECOND CONSTRUCTION PERIOD

1919–21		"Haus Vreede" (private house), Arlesheim
1919–20		"Haus van Blommestein" (Artist's dwelling and studio)
1920–1		Three "Eurythmy Houses"
1921–2		"Haus de Jaager" (Artist's dwelling and studio)
1921		"Haus Friedwart" (hostel). Architect: Paul Bay
1921		"Transformatorenhaus"
1922	New Year's Eve	First Goetheanum destroyed by fire

THIRD CONSTRUCTION PERIOD

1923–4		"Eurythmeum"
1923–4		Extensions to "Haus Brodbeck"
1923–4		"Verlagshaus"
1924	mid-March	Exterior model of the second Goetheanum
1924	9 September	Building permit
1924–5		Site cleared and construction work commences
1924–5		"Haus Schuurman" (composer's dwelling)
1925	30 March	Death of Rudolf Steiner
1926	29 September	Topping-out ceremony
1927	29 September	The wooden statue is erected in the eastern part of the building
1928	29 September	Opening of the second Goetheanum (still incomplete)
1930		Southern staircase and vestibule. Designed by Carl Kemper
1935	Easter	Completion of the room for the wooden statue. Design Meta Pyle-Waller, O. Moser.
1935–6		Alterations and extensions to the "Rudolf Steiner Halde" (former "Haus Brodbeck"). Architect-in-charge: Ernst Aisenpreis

FOURTH CONSTRUCTION PERIOD

1952	Completion of the former rehearsal stage on the ground floor as a hall for 500 persons, with its own stage ("Grundsteinsaal" or Foundation Stone Hall). Architect: Albert von Baravalle
1956–7	Completion of the main auditorium ("Grosser Saal") after previous two-stage competition. Architect: Johannes Schöpfer
1957 Easter	Opening of the completed "Grosser Saal"
1962–4	Western completion. Architects: Rex Raab and Arne Klingborg
1964 Michaelmas	Opening of the west entrance
1969–71	South-eastern completion. Alterations to the south entrance and vestibule. Creation of the "Englischer Saal" (English Lecture Hall). Architect: Rex Raab
1971 Autumn	Murals in the "Englischer Saal": Gerard Wagner

Where not otherwise stated, Rudolf Steiner's designs were executed during the first, second and third construction periods. Under the fourth construction period, only work on the Goetheanum itself is included. Since it was opened in 1928, only a limited amount of buildings (living accommodation, studios, jewellers' training workshops, food research laboratory, students' hostel) have been erected in the immediate vicinity of the Goetheanum.

A general development plan is being passed at the time of going to press. This will allow of an ordered expansion in accordance with the growing needs of the School of Spiritual Science.

THOSE ACTIVE ON THE BUILDING SITE

There follows a list of the craftsmen working in Dornach between 1924 and 1929 during the construction of the second Goetheanum, according to their trade and order of employment.

Masons

Winzeler, Theodor
Geiss, Loric
Sala, Giorgio
Wilhelm, Emil
Grienger, Gottlieb
Wagner, Albert
Fricker, Benjamin
Pilotti, Joseph
Saladin, Oskar
Ammann, Fritz
Nebel, Xaver
Vögtlin, Werner
Brunner, Karl
Luterbacher, Armin
Bauer, Ludwig
Meier, Albin
Ueberreich, Alvis
Dubach, Joseph
Hofer, Joseph

Blast workers

Hänggi, Richard
Kölliker, August
Hänggi, Sylphon

Carpenters

Sonderegger, Emil
Dollinger, Hans
Gosteli, Erwin
Zimmer, Wilhelm
Muespach, Otto
Schaffner, Ernst
Degen, Leo
Gisy, Ferdinand
Kawedon, Josef
Himmelsbach, Karl
Zähringer, Paul
Aleg, Franz
Förler, Karl

Frick, Karl
Zuberbühler, Johann
Mathys, Fritz
Staudenmaier, Michael
Kalt, Ernst
Gschwind, Theophil
Weilenmann, Alfred
Hänny, Fritz
Kurt, Gottlieb
Güetli, Richard
Dunkel, Ernst
Baumann, Arthur
Flubacher, Jacob
Murawski, Friedrich
Weisskopf, Werner
Haibel, Joseph
Barth, Ferdinand
Fleischli, Leopold
Erni, Nikolaus
Kaufmann, Jacob
Wessbecher, Eduard
Zumsteg, Edwin
Bachmann, Hans
Uhlmann, Fritz
Huber, August
Heinzen, Oskar
Schmidt, Theo
Ackermann, Hans
Wittmeier, Otto
Lange, Waldemar
Laich, Johann
Albert, Wilhelm
Strub, Reinhard
Müller, Anton
Dill, Walter
Ackermann, Alfred
Dopllar, Rudolf
Ryser, Ferdinand
Schmalz, Fritz
Hansen, Paul
Möller, Adolf
Eichblatt, Albert
Niese, Richard
Diebold, Friedrich
Bärtschi, Otto
Brun, Jean
Meury, Hermann
Nussbaum, Georg

Hess, Hans
Wohlwend, Paul
Goosz, Elias
Scherer, Otto
Eggli, Anton
Locker, Vitus
Eyberg, Gottlieb
Ivan, Arthur
Volkardt, Gottlieb
Vogt, Wilhelm
Böhurler, Johann
Swinty, Hermann
Bauer, Christian
Lindner, Rudolf
Goosz, Johann
Keller, Karl
Santner, Joseph
Kern, Jacob
Itin, Emil
Bögli, Albert
Eschbach, Carl
Saladin, Hermann
Kern, Gustav
Lange, Waldemar
Stadelmann, Jacob
Meury, Werner, jun.
Nega, Ignaz
Boren, Eduard
Rohr, Adolf
Allgäuer, Franz
Zehnle, Albert
Strub, Reinhard
Kastner, Fritz
Endt, Walter
Stuber, Richard
Gruber, Joseph
Gebs, Hans
Jockum, Jacob
Sux, Theodor
Grössing, Michael
Weiss, Wilhelm
Seldmeyer, Friedrich
Baer, Ernst
Lüdemann, Willi
Gutzwiler, Carl
Schaub, Albert
Männel, Alfred
Rollat, Marc

Eigenmann, Paul
Huber, Rudolf
Oswald, Johann
Thrakl, Joseph
Bächli, Hans
Tobler, Peter
Dollinger, Hans
Gasser, Eugen
Baier, Hans
Sigg, Jakob
Schükli, Joseph
Staufacher, Fritz
Muttenzer, Alexander
Rickenbacher, Heinrich

Steelfixers

Guanella, Albino
Guanella, Luigi
Sigg, Joseph
Zerbini, Ottilio
Zanetti, Francesco
Pacciarelli, Pietro
Dorizzi, Luigi
Gozzi, Gianetto
Sigg, Gebhard
Piovesan, Raimondo
Iovesan, Fortunato
Zanella, Giovanni
Gaetano, Areno
Rotzler, Albert
Hiltbrunner, Christian
Tenti, Carlo
Moraindi, Adolfo
Crolinico, Carlo
Zerbini, Alfonso
Gangler, Paul
Saladin, Beda
Beck, Carl
Tschudin, Carl
Lohm, Ernst
Zuckli, Othmar
Sigg, Ferdinand
Schweizer, Carl
Adimico, Karl

Joiners

Burle, Karl
Wagner, Gustav

Faller, Josef
Müller, Rudolf
Hausmann, Ernst
Schneider, Hermann
Völlmin, Rudolf
Schmidlin, Wilhelm
Anklin, Ernest
Weber-Häuer, Hans
Schulze, Heinrich
Kern, Josef
Grellinger, Achilles
Wagner, Ernst
Hauri, Fritz
Widmer, Carl
Wegelin, Hermann
Degen, Fritz
Grünig, Adolf
Schäfer, Fridolin
Juchli, Paul
Karrer, Werner
Keller, Otto
Eiber, Max
Moser, Walter
Rauh, Albert
Erbsmehl, Jakob
Hänsli, Pius
Imhof, Heinrich
Neugert, Johann
Camenisch, Fritz

Various building trades
Günther, Adam
Flückiger, Arthur
Mejer, Alfons
Dollinger, Nikolaus
Rieder, Peter
Nebel, Otto
Völlmin, Granogott
Seefeld, Wilhelm
Wegelin, Hermann
Bollinger, Fritz

Labourers
Ehrsam, Ernst
Gränicher, Fritz
Meier, Alois
Frei, Simon
Meier, Emil
Meier, Eduard
Gränicher, Walter
Stalder, Albert
Ehrsam, Walter
Meier, Gottfried
Erbsmehl, Paul
Müller, Albert
Schindelholz, Ernst
Schüpbach, Gottfried
Mathys, Werner
Berger, Albert

Ehrsam, Alois
Schwaninger, Arnold
Gerber, Gottlieb
Geiger, Walter
Forrer, Heinrich
Diewald, Charles
Erard, Josef
Vögtli, Emil
Vögtli, Oskar
Gasser, Hermann
Leuthardt, Martin
Saladin, Othmar
Vogel, Joseph
König, Georg
Maeder, Samuel
Meier, Otto
Wiss, Christian
Wiesler, Hans
Ramp, Max
Vögtli, Joseph
Ritzler, Adelbart
Maeder, Fritz
Hochuli, Emil
Bill, Ernst
Bortoli de, Paul
Pfund, Robert
Schmidlin, August
Rickenbach, Daniel
Schmidlin, Hermann
Trüssel, Emil
Schmitz, Peter
Müller, Walter
Trümpi, Heinrich
Vogel, Otto
Dirr, Karl
Schmidlin, Heinrich
Hodel, Ernst
Schmidlin, Wilhelm
Meier, Theodor
Sarasin, Paul
Schmidlin, Robert
Schnabel, Friedrich
Pflugi, Oskar
Billinger, Emil
Chappuis, Arni
Saladin, Lucien
Ambrosi, Josef
Hügli, Simon
Steffen, Fritz
Schmitz, Jean
Schmidlin, Arnold
Müller, Karl
Kessler, Otto
Ditzler, Johann
Wirz, Rudolf
Kunz, Edmund
Wiss, Christian
Meier, Konrad
Brunner, Karl

Aeschlimann, Victor
Hindenlang, Eduard
Schaub, Severin
Löw, Albert
Walser, Richard
Burger, Otto
Scherb, Karl
Latscha, Gustav
Sommer, Otto
Badertscher, Ernst
Nebel, Otto
Born, Richard
Jeger, Fridolin
Trüssel, Emil
Gut, Johann
Nüesch, Alfred
Vogel, Ernst
Hunziker, Karl
Schäfer, Albin
Wolf, Jakob
Vögtli, Otto
Tschmuy, Johann
Wenger, Ignaz
Vögtli, Emil
Mönch, Karl
Müller, Heinrich
Zahnd, Ernst
Renz, Alphons
Währy, Benjamin
Kopp, Reinhard
Feser, Karl
Kohler, Charles
Biasi de, Aurelio
Hunziker, Adolf
Lüber, Walter
Mesmer, Paul
Freiburghaus, Hermann
Rebmann, Hans
Lang, Alois
Zinder, Eduard
Nussbaum, Emil
Krattiger, Hans
Hägler, Hans
Gyger, Johann
Anovi, Anton
Stingelin, Karl
Gloor, Wilhelm
Feigenwinter, Virgil
Dill, Ludwig
Meier, Jacob
Fiechter, Hermann
Erard, Leo
Pianezzi, Cherubino
Urech, Eduard
Albiez, Gustav
Hunziker, Josef
Basso, Karl
Marti, Josef
Lottenbach, Karl

Saladin, Paul
Sommer, Jacob
Graf, Xaver
Schneider, Ernst
Bernasconi, Lois
Hänggi, Josef
Kuhn, Albert
Bosch, Hans
Kälin, Josef
Schumacher, Hans
Lovat, Johann
Straumann, Eduard
Meier, Adelreich
Mathys, Erwin
Fricker, Otto
Kölliker, Louis
Vögtli, Ambrosius
Henzi, Adolf
Sommer, Arnold
Winiger, Victor
Mühlethaler, Albert
Fleury, Stephan
Scherp, Arnold
Schaub, Eduard
Thomann, Joseph
Hügli, Otto
Reinhardt, Arnold
Weiss, Karl
Güetlin, Josef
Stingelin, Hans
Bloch, Johann
Angst, Salomon
Beuchat, Edmond
Vogel, Otto
Diether, Otto
Bieli, Robert
Hänger, Jacob
Stump, Heinrich
Bürgi, Albert
Hügli, Adolf
Bürgi, Walter
Ehrenbogen, Joseph
Maurer, Ernst
Buch, Hans
Stefano, Danioli
Canerri, Federico
della Vecchia, Plinio
Keller, Ernst
Buni (Burri?), Werner
Metzger, Adolf
Bürgi, Paul
Jolidan, Otto
Born, Reinhart
Gatti, Giovanni
Zimmermann, Hans
Weber, Karl
Brunner, Emil
Schaffner, Robert
Müller, Walter

Schmid, Joseph
Frieden, Otto
Stadler, Wilhelm
Herberger, Fritz
Müller, Robert
Pfirter, Wilhelm
Dürring, Fritz
Schauli, Walter
Ruffieux, Joseph
Giesin, Robert
Laup, Hans
Pfirter, Otto
Hartmann, Emil
Wolf, Oswald
Hunziker, Jacob
Gisin, Emil
Fiechter, Ernst
Hostettler, Friedrich
Weisskopf, Fritz
Kaiser, Hans
Huggel, Alphons
Meier, Achilles
Jost, Eduard
Roth, Fritz
Pflugi, Emil
Probst, Fritz
Erni, Karl
Dill, Theophil
Saladin, Rudolf
Schäuble, Hans
Vögtlin, Werner
Karrer, Otto
Fiechter, Wilhelm
Bühlmann, Albert
Steiner, Hans
Kupferschmied, Ernst
Schmid, Andreas
Schmidt, Karl
Nobs, Hans
Schneider, Georg
Kunz, Clemens
Bitterlin, Hermann
Nänny, Christian
Meier, Johann
Kunz, Theophil
Hauswirt, Gustav
Gutzwiller, Alfred
Huber, Luis
Heller, Max
Sparr, Albert
Rolli, Alfred
Kägi, Jacob
Gebus, Ignaz
Oberholzer, Joseph
Bourgeois, Eduard
Kopfmehl, Otto
Vonesch, Louis
Götz, Erwin
Gander, Andreas

Binderli, Martin
Bertschinger, Alfred
Wisard, Edmund
Bläsi, Albert
Haas, Otto
Grieshaber, Albert
Schmidlin, Hans
Fringeli, Severin
Hediger, Robert
Weidmann, Otto
Gantzer, Ernst
Krüsi, Albert
Pallarini, Angelo
Blättler, Karl
Weisskopf, Paul
Basler, Jakob
Moser, Emil
Lingin, Karl
Ruck, Carl
Boder, Werner
Thouvay, Rene
Stracke, Victor
Huber, Joseph
Gerster, Ernst
Vögtli, Theodor
Zihlmann, Peter
Breguard, Paul
Rohrer, Fridolin
Stücki, Constantin
Kunz, Hermann
Kyburg, Carl
Hartmann, Hans
Kunz, Albert
Goetschi, Joseph
Cerry, Camillo
Zönzli, Paul
Meier, Peter
Ammann, Robert
Messerli, Johann
Frey, Albert
Huber, Edwin
Walser, Hans
Hof, Theodor
Bader, Leo
Meyer, Julius
Zahner, Hermann
Dollinger, Otto
Grütter, Eduard
Arnaldini, Heinrich
Meier, Otto
Portner, Leo
Muttenzer, Walter
Argast, Albert
Keiser, Hans
Bernasconi, Luis
Schmidt, Werner
Muespach, Max
Hensch, Emil
Kunz, Emil

Faller, Alfred
Brunella, Carlo
Borer, Linus
Hügli, Otto
Schmidli, Robert
Meier, Constantin
Stegmüller, Emil
Glanzmann, Benedict
Chouvay, René
Fuhrer, Fritz
Kunz, Maurice
Bosshard, Ernst
Gherri, Aurelio
Lang, Hans
Lardon, Carl
Fischer, Rudolf
Fischer, Albert
Vögtli, Paul
Miesch, Otto
Ritter, Fritz
Looser, Werner
Bläsi, Albert
Grüther, Eduard
Zihlmann, Peter
Cantaloppi, Hermann
Nägelin, Ernst
Vögtli, Arthur
Ehrsam, Karl
Probst, Ludwig
Muchenberger, Benjamin
Schnell, August
Weiss, Ferdinand
Wehrle, Alois
Meier, Johann
Bässi, Arnold
Affentranger, Willi
Madörin, Walter
Fischer, Hermann
Meyer, Otto
Ackli, Johann
Lüscher, Alfred
Oehringer, Rudolf
Paulin, Emil
Frinzeli, Emil
Stöcklin, Ernst
Hänggi, Karl
Steiner, Hans
Oser, Ludwig
Oser, Adelbert
Schaulin, Max
Hauswirth, Ernst
Ruetsch, Trowin
Jost, Hans
Wahrer, Emil
Sperb, Arnold
Kohler, Gottfried
Saladin, Othmar
Huber, Fritz
Zumsteg, Edmund

Gersthauer, Fritz
Gränicher, Walter
Oehninger, Rudolf
Hofmeier, Oskar
Meier, Ludwig
Fischer, Albert
Ditzler, Joseph
Borer, Alfred
Kunz, Adolf
Scherer, Otto
Schmidli, Alois
Zihlmann, Peter
Schmidli, Ludwig
Erard, Leo
Kohler, Karl
Chatelain, Albert
Vögtlin, Joseph
Müller, Wilhelm
Götz, Albert
Huber, Fritz
Meier, Konrad
Huber, Fritz
Nebel, Joseph
Huber, Emil
Ehrsam, Werner
Niefergold, Jakob
Zeisy, Gustav
Brülhart, Peter
Aegerter, Wilhelm
Stöcklin, Ernst
Mejer, Alfons
Mäder, Emil
Hartmann, Fritz
Schüpbach, Fritz
Gnetlin, Joseph
Studer, Ernst
Cartier, Arthur
Oser, Ludwig
Seiler, Joseph
Kunz, Joseph
Straumann, Emil
Grütter, Eduard
Schäfer, Ludwig
Nebel, Beat
Schäfer, Karl
Meier, Joseph
Eichenberger, Gottlieb
Zeltner, Moritz
Eggert, Adolf
Christ, Franz
Saladin, Emil
Saladin, Othmar
Christ, Joseph
Berger, Joseph
Meier, Otto
Schmidlin, Robert
Biefer, Emil

BIBLIOGRAPHY

The following list is simply intended as an aid to the study indicated in *Future Prospect* and makes no claim to completeness. Most of the writings and lectures taken from the works of Rudolf Steiner refer wholly or in part to architecture and allied subjects.

RUDOLF STEINER

1888, 9 November
Goethe as Founder of a New Science of Aesthetics, Anthroposophical Publishing Co., London, 1922.

1907, 13 September
The Creative Cosmic Tone, lecture in *Occult Signs and Symbols*, Anthroposophic Press, New York, 1972.

1909, 28 October
"The Being of the Arts", in *1979 Golden Blade*, Rudolf Steiner Press, London, 1979.

1909
An Outline of Occult Science, Chapter IV: Man and the Evolution of the World; Rudolf Steiner Press, London, 1963.

1911, 12 December
And the Temple Becomes Man, Rudolf Steiner Press, London, 1979.

1914, 23 January
Ueber die Anthroposophenkolonie in Dornach.

1914
Ways to a New Style in Architecture, Anthroposophical Publishing Co., London, and Anthroposophic Press, New York, 1927.

7 June	"The Acanthus Leaf."
17 June	"The House of Speech" (Dedication of the Studios where the glass windows were made).
28 June	"The New Conception of Architecture."
5 July	"True Aesthetic Laws of Form."
26 July	"The Creative World of Colour."

1914
Der Dornacher Bau als Wahrzeichen künstlerischer Umwandlungsimpulse, Dornach, 1937.

10 October	"Das Wesen der Geschichte."
18 October	"Die Formen der Säulen und ihr Zusammenhang mit den Grundimpulsen der Kulturepochen."
19 October	"Der Zusammenhang der 5. und 6. Säule mit den Impulsen der mittel- und osteuropäischen Kultur."
24 October	"Architektonische Motive als Erlebensformen. Die Willens-, Gefühls- und Denksphäre des Baus."
25 October	"Die Malerei der grossen Kuppel. Die Baukunst als Sprache der Zukunft."

1914, 28 December
"Technology and Art", in *1959 Golden Blade*, Rudolf Steiner Press, London, 1959.

1914, 29 and 30 December
"The Impulse of Transformation for the Artistic Evolution of Mankind", in *Art in the Light of Mystery Wisdom*, Rudolf Steiner Press, London, 1970.

1915, 1 January
"Artistic and Moral Experience", in *Colour*, Rudolf Steiner Publishing Co., London, and Anthroposophic Press, New York, 1935.

1915, 2 and 4 January
"Plastisch-architektonisches Bilden", in *Kunst im Lichte der Mysterienweisheit*, Dornach, 1974.

1916, 11 January
The Mission of Spiritual Science and of Its Building at Dornach, Switzerland, (published by) H. J. Heywood-Smith, London, 1917.

1916, 20 September
Architectural Forms Considered as the Thoughts of Culture and World-perception, Rudolf Steiner Publishing Co., London (no date).

1918, 15 January
Wesen und Bedeutung der illustrativen Kunst, Dornach, 1940.

1918, 5 May
"Die Quellen der künstlerischen Phantasie und die Quellen der übersinnlichen Erkenntnis", in *Kunst und Kunsterkenntnis*, Dornach, 1961.

1919, 28 October
"Cultural Questions", in *The Social Future*, Anthroposophic Press, New York, 1972.

1920, 8 September
"Die zwölf Sinne des Menschen in ihrer

Beziehung zu Imagination, Inspiration und Intuition", in *Geisteswissenschaftliche Erkenntnis der Grundimpulse sozialer Gestaltung*, Dornach, 1967.

1920, 12 August
"Der übersinnliche Ursprung des Künstlerischen", in *Kunst und Kunsterkenntnis*, Dornach, 1961.

1920
Der Baugedanke von Dornach, Dornach, 1942.

2 October   "Der Bau als Umrahmung der Mysterienspiele."
9 October   "Die den Baugedanken tragenden künstlerischen Impulse."
16 October   "Der Doppelkuppelraum und seine Innenarchitektur."

1921, 29 June
The Architectural Conception of the Goetheanum, Rudolf Steiner Publishing Co., London, and Anthroposophic Press, New York, 1938 (to be used with illustrations from *Der Baugedanke des Goetheanum*, Dornach, 1932).

1921, 29 July
"Architektonische Stilfragen", in *Die Drei* 1930/31, 10th Year, Book 7.

1921
Stilformen des Organisch-Lebendigen, Dornach, 1933.

28 December   "Gestaltung der schaffenden Kräfte der Natur."
30 December   "Die Kunst, eine Offenbarung geheimer Naturgesetze."

1922, 7–12 April
Die Bedeutung der Anthroposophie im Geistesleben der Gegenwart, Dornach, 1957.
Of these six lectures, two have been published in English in the *1961 Golden Blade*:
8 April   "The Position of Anthroposophy among the Sciences."
9 April   "Anthroposophy and the Visual Arts."

1923, 7 January
"Die Herz-Erkenntnis des Menschen", in *Die Not nach dem Christus*, Dornach, 1942.

1923, 19 January
"Truth, Beauty, Goodness", in *Art in the Light of Mystery Wisdom*, Rudolf Steiner Press, London, 1970.

1923, 18 May–9 June
The Arts and Their Mission, Anthroposophic Press, New York, 1964.

1924
"Der Wiederaufbau des Goetheanums", in *Der Goetheanumgedanke inmitten der Kulturkrisis der Gegenwart (Gesammelte Aufsätze)*, Dornach, 1961.

OTHER AUTHORS

Agematsu, Yuji
"Steiner's Art at the Goetheanum", *The Geijutsu-Shincho*, No. 4/1971, Tokyo.

Architectural Design
Concrete Interlude, July 1971, London.

Architectural Forum
An Architect's Scrapbook: The secret dossier of an architectural scavenger, New York, 1964.

Architectural Institute of Japan, Transactions of
On the Architecture of Rudolf Steiner, No. 186/1971, Tokyo.

Architects
Rudolf Steiner's Architecture. No. 26/1963, Copenhagen.

Bücher, Max and Erwin Heinle
Building in Visual Concrete, Technical Press, London, 1967.

Baravalle, Albert
"Das Goetheanum in Dornach", in *Schweizerische Technische Zeitschrift*, No. 42/1945.
"Das Form-Motiv des Zweiten Goetheanum", in *Das Goetheanum*, No. 12, 31st Year, 1952.

Bayes, Kenneth
"Architecture in Accord with Man", in *The Faithful Thinker: Centenary Essays on the Work and Thought of Rudolf Steiner*, Hodder and Stoughton, London, 1961.

Bauwelt 1962
Diskussion über das Westtreppenhaus des zweiten Goetheanums.

Bonfanti, Enzio, and Mario Porta
"L'architettura: Fondazione del movimento moderno", in *L'Arte moderna*, No. 123, Vol. XIV, Milan, 1967.

Brion-Guerry, L.
L'Année 1913, Vol. 2, Editions Klincksieck, Paris, 1971.

Brunato, Mario, and Sandro Mendini
L'Architettura, Nos. 55, 56, 57, 58. Rome, 1960.

Conrads, Ulrich, and H. H. Sperlich
"Ueber Steiners Dornacher Bauten", in *Phantastische Architektur*, Ullstein, Berlin, 1960.

Fant, Åke, Arne Klingborg, and A. John Wilkes
Rudolf Steiner's Sculpture in Dornach, Rudolf Steiner Press, London, 1975.

Fiechter, Ernst
"Zum Neubau des Goetheanums bei Dornach", in *Schweizerische Bauzeitung*, Vol. 85, No. 7/1925.

Gessner, Wolfgang
Die Sprache der Baukunst, Raum und Gebärde, Verlag Freies Geistesleben, Stuttgart, 1948.
Baukunst in der Wende der Zeit, Verlag Freies Geistesleben, Stuttgart, 1956.
Das zweite Goetheanum und der Baugedanke, Verlag Freies Geistesleben, Stuttgart, 1965.

Gubler, Jacques
"Beton et architecture, Trois propositions des années 1925", in *Werk*, 5/1971, Zürich.

Hartmann, Georg
The Goetheanum Glass-Windows, Philosophisch-Anthroposophischer Verlag, Dornach, 1972.

Hemleben, Johannes
Rudolf Steiner, Henry Goulden Ltd, East Grinstead, 1976.

Hitchcock, Henry-Russell
Architecture – Nineteenth and Twentieth Centuries, Penguin Books, London, 1958.

Ikehara, Joshiro
"Introducing Eminent Works, Goetheanum at Dornach", in *Space Design*, No. 15/1966, Tokyo.

Imai, Kenji

"Gaudi and Steiner", in *Glass and Architecture*, No. 3/1964, Tokyo.
Rudolf Steiner and his Works, Kindaikenchiku 5, Tokyo, 1964.
"Augenzeuge der modernen Architektur". Schweiz 1926. *Shinkenchiku*, July 1971, Tokyo.

Kayser, Felix

Architektur heute und morgen, Verlag Die Kommenden, Freiburg, 1969.

Kemper, Carl

Der Bau, Verlag Freies Geistesleben, Stuttgart, 1966.

Meissner Reese, Ilse

"Steiner's Goetheanum at Dornach", in *Progressive Architecture*, September 1965, New York.

Pehnt, Wolfgang

Expressionist Architecture, Thames and Hudson, London, 1973.

Raab, Rex

"Rudolf Steiner und die Baukunst", in *Bauwelt*, No. 7/1964, Berlin.
"Eurythmie und Mysteriendramen im Goetheanum zu Dornach", in *Bühnentechnische Rundschau*, 1/1965, Berlin.
"Bedeutung und Aufgabe der Farbe im Schulbau", in *Das Deutsche Malerblatt*, No. 19/1969, Stuttgart.
"Möbel für Menschen am Beispiel Tisch und Stuhl", in *Der Deutsche Schreiner*, No. 11/1969, Stuttgart.
"Architecture — Buildings for Life", in *Work Arising from the Life of Rudolf Steiner*, Rudolf Steiner Press, London, 1975.

Ranzenberger, Hermann

"Das neue Goetheanum, ein Eisenbetonbau", in *Westdeutsche Bau-Schau*, 1st December 1926.

Rath, Wilhelm

The Imagery of the Goetheanum Windows, Rudolf Steiner Press, London, 1976.

Rotzler, Willy

"Das Goetheanum in Dornach als Beispiel der Integration der Künste", in *Werk*, No. 8/1960, Zürich.

Sharp, Dennis

"Rudolf Steiner and the Way to a New Style in Architecture", in *Architectural Association Journal*, June 1963, London.
Modern Architecture and Expressionism, Longmans Green, London, 1966.
"Thoughts of Love in a Concrete Climate", in the *Guardian*, October 1971.

Turgenieff, Assya

The Goetheanum Windows, Rudolf Steiner Publishing Co., London, and Anthroposophic Press, New York, 1938.

Werk

60 Jahre Schweizer Architektur, January 1968, Zürich.

Wyssling, W.

"Zum Neubau des Goetheanums bei Dornach", in *Schweizerische Bauzeitung*, Vol. 85, No. 7.

Zimmer, Erich

Rudolf Steiner als Architekt von Wohn- und Zweckbauten, Verlag Freies Geistesleben, Stuttgart, 1970.

LIST OF ILLUSTRATIONS

106   "Haus Duldeck". Rudolf Steiner's wax model for the main entrance to the north-west. 1914.

107   "Haus Duldeck". Main entrance to the north-west, as executed.

108   "Haus Duldeck". Front facing the Goetheanum, from the north.

109   "Haus Duldeck" from the north-east.

110   "Haus Duldeck" from the west.

111   "Haus Duldeck". Detail of south-east front.

112   "Haus de Jaager". Rudolf Steiner's original model. 1920.

113   "Haus de Jaager" from the north-west.

114   "Haus de Jaager". Working model from the north.

115   "Haus de Jaager". Detail of north entrance.

116   The "Eurythmeum" from the north-east.

117   The "Eurythmeum". Detail of north-east entrance.

118   The "Eurythmeum" from the east.

119, 120, 121   The "Eurythmeum". Rudolf Steiner's plasticine model.

122   The "Eurythmeum" from the south-west. To the right, the old "Haus Brodbeck".

123   The "Eurythmeum". Detail from north-east.

124   The "Eurythmeum" from the south-west. To the right, the old "Haus Brodbeck".

125   The "Eurythmeum". Detail from south-west.

126   Panorama of the Dornach hill from the north.

127   The Goetheanum. Western staircase at terrace level.

128, 129   The Goetheanum. Terrace in the west during an interval.